THE FAILURE OF THE UNITED NATIONS DEVELOPMENT PROGRAMS FOR AFRICA

Adrien M. Ratsimbaharison

University Press of America,® Inc.
Dallas · Lanham · Boulder · New York · Oxford

Copyright © 2003 by
University Press of America,® Inc.
4501 Forbes Boulevard
Suite 200
Lanham, Maryland 20706
UPA Acquisitions Department (301) 459-3366

PO Box 317
Oxford
OX2 9RU, UK

Library of Congress Control Number: 2003112592
ISBN 0-7618-2668-8 (paperback : alk. ppr.)

∞™ The paper used in this publication meets the minimum
requirements of American National Standard for Information
Sciences—Permanence of Paper for Printed Library Materials,
ANSI Z39.48—1984

Contents

List of Figures

List of Tables

List of abbreviations

AAF-SAP	African Alternative Framework to Structural Adjustment Programmes for Socio-Economic Recovery and Transformation.
ACP	African, Caribbean and Pacific.
AEC	African Economic Community.
APPER	Africa's Priority Programme for Economic Recovery, 1986-1990.
AREMA	Avant-Garde de le Revolution Malgache.
BFV	Banky Fampandrosoana ny Varotra (Bank for the Development of Trade).
BTM	Bankin' ny Tantsaha Mpamokatra (Bank for the Farmers).
CBI	Cross Border Initiative.
COMESA	Common Market for Eastern and Southern Africa.
DCPE	Document Cadre de la Politique Economique (Economic Policy Framework Document)
EC	European Community.
ECA (or UNECA)	United Nations Economic Commission of Africa.
ELG	Export-led growth.
EPZ	Export Processing Zone.
EU	European Union.
FDI	Foreign Direct Investment.
GDP	Gross Domestic Product.
GNP	Gross National Product.
IMF	International Monetary Fund.
ISI	Import-substituting industrialization.
LDC	Least Developed Country.
LPA	Lagos Plan of Action.

MEDIA	Mauritius Export Development and Investment Authority.
MLP	Mauritian Labour Party.
MMM	Mouvement Militant Mauricien.
MNC	Multinational Corporation.
MSM	Mouvement Socialiste Mauricien.
NIC	Newly Industrialized Country.
NIEO	New International Economic Order.
OAU	Organisation of African Unity.
OECD	Organisation for Economic Co-operation and Development.
ODA	Official Development Assistance.
PSD	Parti Social Democrate.
PSM	Parti Socialiste Mauricien.
SAP	Structural Adjustment Program.
SDR	Special Drawing Rights.
SOLIMA	Solitany Malagasy (Malagasy Petroleum Company).
TNC	Transnational Corporation.
UN	United Nations.
UNCTAD	United Nations Conference on Trade and Development.
UNDD	Union National pour la Democratie et le Developpement,
UNDP	United Nations Development Programme.
UNESCO	United Nations Educational, Scientific and Cultural Organization.
UNECA (or ECA) United Nations Economic Commission of Africa.
UNICEF	United Nations Children's Fund.
UNIDO	United Nations Industrial Development Organization.
UNNADAF	United Nations New Agenda for the Development of Africa in the 1990s.
UNPAAERD	United Nations Programme of Action for the African Economic Recovery and Development 1986-1990.

Foreword

by Donald J. Puchala

Adrien Ratsimbaharison's *The Failure of the United Nations Development Programs for Africa* is a useful, timely, and most welcome contribution to our better understanding of the workings of the United Nations. The study offers an honest appraisal of the politics of development that especially within the UN have hampered poorer countries much more than helped them. Not very many development analysts, and even fewer African scholars, have been forthright enough to say what Ratsimbaharison says in his book. This is that the development dialogue within the UN has been much more about ideologically charged politics than about sound economics. And while it is politically less than correct these days to say anything praiseworthy about the structural adjustment prescriptions of the World Bank and the International Monetary Fund, Ratsimbaharison here too refuses to conform. In terms of development results, structural adjustment has a rather impressive track record, and Ratsimbaharison acknowledges this. The main findings of Ratsimbaharison's study are controversial. Yet, there is nothing about the book that is polemical. Its conclusions follow from the careful analysis of an enormous collection of United Nations documents. Following the complex and convoluted paper trail is the only reliable way to work one's way through the maze and haze of decision-making within the United Nations. Ratsimbaharison does this expertly and exhaustively. Those who might like to take issue with his findings are challenged to display their evidence in the qualities and quantities that Ratsimbaharison attains. To make his points, Ratsimbaharison is also obliged to examine the "real world" outside the United Nations so that he might compare and contrast it with the surreal world that frequently prevails inside. He makes this comparison in two in-depth case studies of African developmental experiences --

Madagascar and Mauritius during the twenty odd years between the mid 1970s and the late 1990s. Both national experiences illustrate rather persuasively that the way not to develop economically during the latter decades of the twentieth century was to comply with the development prescriptions of the United Nations. This seemed to be particularly the case regarding Africa, but the lessons are more general.

There is among practitioners and analysts alike at present a widespread acknowledgement that the main axis of political contention within the United Nations is North vs. South, or better said, South vs. North. The UN is the place where the poorer countries of the world make demands on the richer countries, and such demands make up most of the agenda of the United Nations General Assembly. Demands for economic justice, for greater equality, for higher standards of living and improved well-being are certainly legitimate, as are requests for assistance and redistribution. But, at the United Nations, such demands tend to be enveloped in ideological accounts of how the poor countries became poor and why many remain that way. Too often at the UN scoring ideological points turns out to be more important than opening pathways to cooperation. This comes through loudly and clearly in Ratsimbaharison's analysis. Even more damaging to economic development are strategies for change based on ideologically derived – and faulty – explanations for existing conditions.

Ratsimbaharison observes and reports on what can only be called the political surrealism of the United Nations General Assembly in the context of formulating *The United Nations Programme of Action for Economic Recovery and Development*, and the subsequent *United Nations New Agenda for the Development of Africa*. The strategies were mapped in accord with faulty assumptions about the causes of deteriorating living standards in many parts of Africa. They were accepted because they coincided with third world political themes voiced in North-South debates; they were adopted by acclamation in the General Assembly because large third world majorities, combined with Northern indifference, rendered voting unnecessary; they were then ignored by Northern governments that found them unpromising in the first place, by Bretton Woods institutions that questioned their economics, and also by the African governments that promoted them. The UN-prescribed development programs for Africa failed almost totally, although committees of the General Assembly never quite recognized this or at least were loath to admit it. Meanwhile, any number of African countries agreed to structural adjustment programs prescribed by the World Bank and the International Monetary Fund, and a number of these countries, like Mauritius, came out the better for their experience.

In a very telling way, Ratsimbaharison explains that the failures of the United Nations, or perhaps better said, the failures of those who promoted the closed-economy, import substituting, statist strategies that became the development plans for Africa, were as much conceptual as political. By the 1980s the globalizing, open, privatizing, liberal world economy could no longer accommodate development thinking reminiscent of the 1960s. The UN of the African development plans was out of sync, both practically and theoretically, with the real political economy of the world.

Fortunately, perhaps, this flawed conceptualization has been altered. The prevailing political-economic thinking of Kofi Annan's United Nations is liberal and globalist. The United Nations today is promoting openness, privatiziation and structural adjustment. The Secretary-General himself is emphasizing partnerships between third world governments and multinational firms, and political taboos that forbade linking economic underdevelopment to ineffective, kleptocratic or corrupt governance have been lifted. Similarly overcome in UN discourse have been hesitations about connecting poverty to human insecurity and underdevelopment to incessant civil warfare. "Neo-colonialism" and "dependency" simply no longer wash as explanations for endemic poverty in Africa or anywhere else. In these ways, the United Nations may be becoming less politically surrealistic than during the periods that Ratsimbaharison writes about. On the other hand, the resistance that Kofi Annan has encountered in his attempts to bring the UN into the liberal world economy suggests that the lessons of Ratsimbaharison's excellent book need to be carefully pondered.

Columbia, South Carolina
March, 2003

Preface

This study attempts to explain why the two major United Nations (UN) development programs for Africa in the 1980s and 1990s (UNPAAERD and UNNADAF) failed to promote economic and social development on the continent. In doing so, it systematically analyzes the two UN development programs, and identifies the internal and external causes of their failure, by focusing on the processes of their formulation, adoption, implementation and evaluation within the UN General Assembly, and discussing their formulation and implementation within the context of the late 20th century world economic order. Furthermore, in order to concretize the theoretical analyses of these programs, this study discusses the development experiences of two African countries (Madagascar and Mauritius), within the context of the formulation and implementation of these programs.

In conclusion, this study suggests that the two UN development programs for Africa failed because of the conjunction of the *institutional weaknesses* of the UN organization itself, and the constraints imposed upon these programs by the *interacting forces within the late 20th century world economic order*. While the *institutional weaknesses* of the UN included its inability to generate potentially effective development programs and to get the compliance of the international community, the *interacting forces within the late 20th century world economic order* were constituted by capitalist material capabilities, liberal ideas and the Bretton Woods institutions.

Acknowledgements

Many people and institutions were involved in the completion of this study, which is a revised and updated version of a Ph.D. dissertation submitted to the Department of Government and International Studies (GINT Department), University of South Carolina, Columbia, SC. First and foremost, I am very grateful to Professor Donald Puchala, former Director of the Richard Walker Institute of International Studies at the University of South Carolina, who accepted to supervise my dissertation and write a very useful foreword for this publication. I would like also to thank the other members of my dissertation committee for their help, insights and dedication: Professor Roger Coate, Professor Janice Love, and Professor John McDermott.

I am also grateful to many other faculty members of the GINT Department, who helped me in one way or another, particularly Professor Mark DeLancey and Professor Mark Tompkins. Of course, none of these people can be held accountable for any mistake contained in this book.

Furthermore, this study also benefited from the financial support from the Fulbright Institution, the GINT Department, the University of South Carolina, and the Strom Thurmond Fellowship in International Relations.

Last, but not least, I want also to thank my wife, Danielle, and my children, Tsilavo and Ony, for their daily support, which gave me strength and inspiration throughout the completion of this study.

Chapter One

Introduction

The United Nations (UN) was created, not only to "maintain international peace and security," but also to "promote social progress and better standards of life."[1]* To this end, the UN was mandated to "employ international machinery for the promotion of the economic and social advancement of *all peoples*."[2] In connection with this mission, the UN proclaimed four "decades of development" from the 1960s to the 1990s, and created a total of 35 multilateral institutions for international development (Gwin, C. and Williams, M. 1996: 111). Moreover, it designed and implemented hundreds of development programs and, at a score of global conferences, issued countless plans of action for the development of developing countries.

With regard to Africa in particular, the UN allocated to the continent more than $1 billion a year in official development assistance (ODA) since 1988 (OECD, various years). Furthermore, in addition to the routine development programs undertaken by virtually all existing UN programs and funds (such as UNDP, UNICEF, UNESCO, UNIDO, etc.), the UN adopted two major programs for the economic recovery and development of Africa: (1) the United Nations Programme of Action for African Economic Recovery and Development, 1986-1990 (UNPAAERD) in 1986,[3] and (2) the United Nations New Agenda for the Development of Africa in the 1990s (UNNADAF) in 1991.[4] These two programs were designed to solve the critical economic and social problems prevailing in Africa since the 1970s, and were based upon the concept of *global compact*.[5]

The concept of *global compact* refers to the mutual agreement

---

* Notes may be found at the end of each Chapter.

between the African countries and the international community, in which, as specified in Resolution S-13/2, the African countries are committed "to launch both national and regional programmes of economic development";[6] and the international community is committed "to support and complement the African development efforts."[7] One of the most important implications of this *global compact* is that all member states of the UN are urged to "take action for the rapid and full implementation" of the development programs[8]; and all organs, organizations and bodies of the UN system are requested to "participate fully in and support" their implementation.[9] In sum, the concept of *global compact* implies collective actions and responsibility of the African countries and the international community.

This study is concerned with the *UN organization*, not with the whole *UN system*. The term *UN organization* refers to the principal organs of the UN (i.e., the General Assembly, the Secretariat, the Security Council, the International Court of Justice, the Economic and Social Council and the Trusteeship Council), and all UN programs and funds whose governing bodies report directly to these principal organs. However, the term *UN system* refers not only to the "UN organization," but also to all specialized agencies (such as the World Bank and the International Monetary Fund) and autonomous organizations (like the International Atomic Energy Agency, IAEA), whose governing bodies do not report directly to the principal organs of the UN organization (Riggs and Plano, 1994: 21-24). This distinction between "UN organization" and "UN system" is very important, because it can be used to explain why most specialized agencies (particularly, the World Bank and the International Monetary Fund) do not generally comply with the decisions of the different organs of the UN organization, especially the resolutions of the UN General Assembly (Riggs and Plano, 1994: 21-22).

The UN and the Economic and Social Development in Africa

Most students of the UN agree that this organization has not performed satisfactorily in the realm of economic and social development (Adams, 1994; Weiss, et al. 1994; DeLancey, 1994; Gwin and Williams, 1996; Puchala, 1996). Particularly, in the case of Africa, Mark DeLancey (1994), while noticing the "powerful omnipresence" of the UN on the continent, notes that:

the UN efforts, even when combined with the efforts of African governments, donor nations, NGOs, etc., have been woefully inadequate to the challenge. The economic, social, and political problems persist, and by some measures worsen, in spite of these activities, projects, and undertakings. (DeLancey, 1994: 296)

More specifically, concerning UNPAAERD, the first UN development program for Africa, the author reports that:

A conference of African government ministers in Addis Ababa in 1991 declared that 'Africa does not need another UNPAAERD.' The program had 'had very little positive impact' and it had failed to rally international assistance. A similar program would only further the marginalization of Africa by separating Africa's problems from those of the world. (DeLancey, 1994: 296-297)

The UN General Assembly itself recognized to some extent the failure of UNPAAERD. Among many different causes of this failure, the final review of the program points to the fact that this program "did not quite become a focal point for economic policy or for resource mobilization on behalf of Africa."[10] Consequently, as the final review of UNPAAERD puts it:

none of the goals of the Programme of Action were fully realized. Targets for growth, food security, human investment and debt reduction were missed, so declines rather than hoped-for increases have been recorded by many States and for Africa as a whole. (UN document A/RES/46/151 of 18 December 1991, annex I.A, parag. 1.)

With regard to UNNADAF, the second UN development program for Africa in the 1990s, the Ad Hoc Committee for the mid-term review of its implementation plainly recognized in 1996 that this program failed to achieve its "primary objectives of transformation, integration, diversification and growth of the African economies."[11] As the Ad Hoc committee put it:

Many of the critical economic and social problems of Africa which led to the adoption by the General Assembly of the United Nations Programme of Action for African Economic Recovery and Development (resolution S-13/2 of 1 June 1986) and of the New Agenda [UNNADAF] in 1991 still exist in 1996. In some countries the problems have even worsened[...]. In Africa poverty and unemployment are expected to increase substantially.

The estimated resource mobilization levels in the New Agenda are still far from being attained and the key development goals have yet to be met. (UN document No. A/51/48 of 27 September 1996, annex I., parag. 4)

Since this 1996 mid-term review, some changes were made concerning the implementation of UNNADAF. However, despite these changes, there was no significant improvement of its effectiveness. Consequently, as the UN Secretary General reported, UNNADAF also failed to address the dramatic economic and social situation of Africa, particularly within the context of globalization:

In the case of Africa, globalization has resulted in a deepening of the continent's marginalization. For example, Africa's trade accounted for only 1.5 per cent of global trade in 1998. Export earnings remain small, having declined from 3.2 per cent of world export revenues in 1985 to 2.3 per cent in 1990 and to 1.5 per cent in 1995. African exports are dominated by agricultural products (primary commodities), rendering the continent's export-earning capacity highly sensitive to commodity price fluctuations. (UN document No. A/55/350 of 15 September 2000, p. 32)

This successive failure of these two UN development programs for Africa was the impetus for this study, which attempts to find out what went wrong with these programs. The question, in its broadest formulation, is why is there such a marked difference between what the UN has intended to do (i.e., ideals of development of *all peoples*, as stated in the UN Charter), and what it has actually achieved (i.e., realities of failed programs). This study will attempt to identify the major obstacles to the success of the two UN development programs. As we will see, these obstacles have to do, on the one hand, with the ways the UN programs were formulated, adopted, and implemented by member states, UN bodies, and other international organizations; and on the other hand, with the international economic system, or the *world economic order*,[12] in which the UN actions in economic and social development take place.

The questions addressed in this study are pertinent, not only in the context of the continuing critical economic and social conditions in most African countries, but also in the context of the debate on UN reform (Childers, 1994; Puchala, 1996). Indeed, a good understanding of the failure of these two UN development programs will help in formulating and implementing better international development programs for the African countries. Furthermore, in order to make the

UN more effective and efficient in economic and social development, we need to know why previous UN development programs failed.

While there is much literature on the critical economic and social conditions in Africa (World Bank, 1981, 1984, 1989 and 1996; Ravenhill, Ed., 1986; Engberg-Pedersen et al., 1996, etc.), very little has been said about the performance of the UN in promoting economic and social development on the continent. Indeed, beyond the general studies on the UN's role in African development (DeLancey, 1994; Nworah, 1975; and Ajaegbo, 1986, 1984 and 1985), and the rhetorical claims by some individuals, like George Ayittey (July 26, 1996), that the UN has done "too little and too late" for Africa, there is no comprehensive study that attempts to systematically assess the UN's performance in this domain.

The existing literature provides, however, two explanations of the poor performance of the UN outside Africa. The first explanation involves internal factors to the world organization, factors that have been described as "intellectual and organizational limits" of the UN (Puchala, 1996), or its "institutional weaknesses" (Gwin and Williams, 1996). The second explanation involves external factors, related to the international system or world order, within which the UN is acting.

Among the authors who emphasize the internal factors, Donald Puchala (1996) explains the failure of the UN to formulate sound development strategies with its "intellectual and organizational limits," which included, among other things, the existence of countless agencies, organs, and sub-organs, with little communication and coordination among them (Puchala, 1996: 233). For their part, Catherine Gwin and Maurice Williams (1996) use the concept of "institutional weaknesses" to describe these intellectual and organizational limits that prevent the UN from being more effective and efficient. According to the authors, these institutional weaknesses involve policy incoherence, program sprawl, agency competition, administrative laxness and governance by member states.[13]

Among the authors who emphasize the external factors, Thomas Weiss et al. (1994) argue that the success of any UN action ultimately depends on the consensus of member states and, most importantly, on the agreement of the "major states" (such as the United States) to let the UN do what it intends to do. In this sense, the authors explain the failure of most UN actions by the fact that this organization does not have the financial resources it needs to implement its policies. In connection with these arguments, Geoff Simons (1995) introduces the concept of "parallel UN," comprised of the coalition of the capitalist developed countries, the World Bank, the International Monetary Fund (IMF), and the multinational corporations (MNC), which exercises powerful constraints on the UN and its weak member states.

The UN as a Development Agency and an International Actor

This study considers the UN as both a development agency making and implementing its own program or policy, as well as an international actor working within the international system. Its main objective is to identify the internal and external causes of the failure of the two UN development programs for Africa in the 1980s and 1990s (UN-PAAERD and UNNADAF). Using the *framework for policy analysis* suggested by William Dunn (1994), it will systematically analyze the two programs, in Chapters 2 and 3. These analyses will set the stage for the identification of the internal causes of the failure of the two UN development programs, in Chapter 4. Next, using the *framework for action* or *historical structure* suggested by Robert W. Cox (1986), in Chapter 5, it will analyze the formulation and implementation of the two UN development programs within the context of the late 20th century world economic order. This second analysis will allow us to identify the external causes of the failure of these two UN development programs.

Compared to other available frameworks for policy analysis (Jones, 1977; Hogwood and Gunn, 1984; among others), Dunn's framework is more appropriate for analyzing international public policies. Indeed, contrary to the other frameworks that are specifically designed for national public policies, it does not involve policy-making processes that hardly exist within the UN, such as legitimation and appropriation processes (Jones, 1977: 84-135). In addition, Dunn's framework is relatively simple and flexible. It focuses on five policy-making processes that are very important within the UN: agenda setting, policy formulation, policy adoption, policy implementation and policy assessment or evaluation. In order to analyze these five policy-making processes, Dunn suggests five procedures of policy analysis: problem structuring, forecasting, recommendation, monitoring and evaluation.

In looking at the UN as an international actor, we found that the mainstream International Relations theories (realism or neo-realism, and idealism, liberalism or neo-liberalism) (Kegley, Ed., 1995; Viotti and Kauppi, 1993; and Dougherty and Pfaltzgraff, 1990) are not very useful for explaining the failure of the UN actions. On the one hand, the focus on the states and their power, in the realist or neo-realist framework, is not adequate to appreciate the importance of international institutions (such as the World Bank, the IMF, etc.), and ideas flowing in the international system (such as liberal or Marxist ideas). On the other hand, the idealist, liberal or neo-liberal assumption about the possibility of progress through cooperation or better institutions does not always fit in the real world. Furthermore, even if we would have to take into account the phenomena of inequality and domination within the international system, we should avoid the crude determinism of Marxist theory and/or dependency theory.

Consequently, in taking into consideration all of the above parameters, we will adopt the *framework for action* or *historical structure* suggested by Robert W. Cox (1986). Based on his personal interpretation of the writings of the Italian activist and philosopher Antonio Gramsci, Cox's *framework for action* is conceived as a "picture of a particular world order," or a picture of "a particular configuration of forces" (Cox, 1986: 217). In this sense, Robert Cox argues that a *world order* "imposes pressures and constraints" on the actions of individual or group members involved in that particular world order (Cox, 1986: 217-218). Specifically, with regard to the *forces interacting* within a particular world order, Robert Cox notes that:

> Three categories of forces (expressed as potentials) interact in a [world order]: *material capabilities, ideas and institutions.* No one-way determinism needs to be assumed among these three; the relationships can be assumed to be reciprocal. (Cox, 1986: 218) (Emphasis added)

Robert Cox (1986) defines *material capabilities* as "productive and destructive potentials," which exist either as "technological and organizational capabilities," or as natural resources, stocks of equipment and wealth. Furthermore, he distinguishes two types of *ideas*: the first type is described as "intersubjective meanings, or shared notions of social relations which tend to perpetuate habits and expectations of behavior"; the second type as "collective images of social order held by different groups of people" (Cox, 1986: 218-219). Finally, Robert Cox defines *institutions* as "amalgams of ideas and material power," which stabilize and perpetuate a world order (Cox, 1986: 218-219).

In this study we consider that the *interacting forces within the late 20ᵗʰ century world economic order* were constituted by capitalist material capabilities, variants of liberal ideas, and the Bretton Woods institutions. Thus, we will analyze the UN actions in development in the context of these interacting forces. It is in this sense that Cox's framework is very interesting, especially in the identification of the external causes of the failure of the UN development programs in Chapter 5.

The Case Studies of Madagascar and Mauritius

Any African country could have been used as a case study to illustrate the failure of the two UN development programs. However, we chose to focus on the cases of Madagascar (Chapter 6) and Mauritius (Chapter 7), because of the similarities of their situation at independence and the big differences in their development experiences throughout the 1980s and 1990s. Madagascar and Mauritius are two island nations off the East coast of Africa. Both countries were members of the Organisation of African Unity (OAU), the Group of 77, and the Non-Aligned Movement. They were poor and did not have a lot of resources at their independence (1960 for Madagascar, and 1971 for Mauritius). Nevertheless, while Madagascar steadily declined throughout much of the 1980s and 1990s and joined the rank of the poorest countries in the world,[14] Mauritius achieved a tremendous economic and social development during the same period, and joined the club of upper-middle-income economies in the 1990s.[15] In both cases, the two UN development programs appeared to be useless, either to get Madagascar out of its trouble, or to help Mauritius sustain high GDP growth rates.

The Concept of Economic and Social Development

Before analyzing the two UN development programs, we need to discuss briefly the concept of *economic and social development*, as it is used in this study. The definitions and operationalizations of this concept have changed and diversified over time. For instance, as we will find out in the following chapters, most African political leaders and policy makers tend to conceive *economic and social development* in terms of *political and economic independence*, as well as in terms of *self-sufficiency and self-reliance*. However, the representatives of developed countries generally define *economic and social development* in terms of *economic growth, increased economic opportunities* and *political freedom*. Furthermore, while the United Nations Development Programme (UNDP) has its own *"human development index"* which combines national income, adult literacy and life expectancy (UNDP, *Human Development Report*, various years), the World Bank uses *per capita income* as the most important indicator of economic and social development (World Bank, *World Development Report*, various years).

Despite all of these different definitions and operationalizations, there are nevertheless some key elements of what we can safely describe as *economic and social development*. First, we have to recognize that economic and social development includes, but is not limited to *economic growth*, which can be measured in terms of annual percentage growth of the gross domestic product (GDP) of a given country. Second, *economic and social development* also means a *process of long-term improvement of the economic and social conditions* of the large majority of the population of a given country. In this sense, it is characterized by "higher standards of living in terms of income, food and other forms of consumption, health, housing, education" (Welsh and Butorin, Ed., 1990). In connection with this definition, the economic and social development of African countries will be measured in terms of annual growth rates of GDP, per capita GNP, life expectancy at birth, and percentage of adult literacy.

Notes

[1] *Charter of the United Nations*, Preamble.

[2] *Ibid.*, (Emphasis added).

[3] UNPAAERD (United Nations Programme of Action for African Economic Recovery and Development, 1986-1990) was adopted by UN General Assembly Resolution S-13/2 of 1 June 1986 (UN document No. A/RES/S-13/2).

[4] UNNADAF (United Nations New Agenda for the Development of Africa in the 1990s) was adopted by UN General Assembly Resolution 46/151 of 18 December 1991 (UN document No. A/RES/46/151) in replacement of UNPAAERD.

[5] UN document No. A/RES/46/151 of 18 December 1991, annex I.A, parag. 2.

[6] UN document No. A/RES/S-13/2 of 1 June 1986, annex II, parag. 8.

[7] *Ibid.*.

---

[8]   *Ibid.*, parag. 3.

[9]   *Ibid.*, parag. 4.

[10]   UN document A/RES/46/151 of 18 December 1991, annex I.A, parag. 1.

[11]   UN document No. A/51/48 of 27 September 1996, annex I.

[12]   We will refer in this study to Robert Cox's definition of *"world orders,"* as "the particular configurations of forces which successively define the problematic of war or peace for the ensemble of states" (Cox, 1986: 220). In this sense, a *world economic order* would be a particular configuration of forces, which would define the problematic of conflict or cooperation in the economic domain for the ensemble of actors in the world economic system.

[13]   In fact, "governance by member states" can be also classified as an external factor.

[14]   According to the World Bank (2001: 33), the per capita GNP of Madagascar declined from $450 in 1980 to $250 in 1999. It was steadily declining at the rate of 2.2 per cent a year since 1985. As a result, Madagascar is now classified by the United Nations and the World Bank as a Least Developed Countries (LDCs), among a group of countries including: Chad, Mozambique, Nepal, Uganda, etc.

[15]   According to the World Bank (2001: 33), the per capita GNP of Mauritius increased from $1240 in 1980 to $3550 in 1999. It was growing at the rate of 5.4 per cent a year since 1985. As a result, Mauritius is now classified by the United Nations and the World Bank as a upper-middle-income economy, among a group of countries including: South Africa, Gabon, Mexico, Brazil, Malaysia, Czech Republic, Greece, etc.

Chapter 2

The United Nations Programme of Action for the African Economic Recovery and Development, 1986-1990 (UNPAAERD)

The UN General Assembly adopted the United Nations Programme of Action for African Economic Recovery and Development, 1986-1990 (UNPAAERD) on June 1, 1986,[1] to address the critical economic and social conditions which prevailed in Africa since the end of the 1970s. The systematic analysis of this first UN development program will lead us to discuss how it was set on the agenda of the UN General Assembly, and how it was formulated, adopted, implemented and evaluated by policy makers and/or stakeholders within and outside the UN.

UNPAAERD and the UN Agenda

In addressing the question of how UNPAAERD was set on the agenda of the UN General Assembly, and how the African economic and social problems of the 1980s were defined by the different groups of policy makers and/or stakeholders within the UN General Assembly, we need to analyze Resolution S-13/2 and its annex containing UNPAAERD, along with the proposals submitted to the UN General Assembly during its 13th Special Session in 1986. As we will see, the different groups of policy makers and/or stakeholders within the UN General Assembly defined the African economic and social problems of the 1980s differently.

Africa was desperately mired in an unprecedented economic and social crisis at the beginning of the 1980s. Describing this crisis in his report to the General Assembly on October 23, 1984, the UN Secretary General pointed out the fact that 27 out of 36 African countries were "facing abnormal food shortage," and nine countries were "severely affected by drought."[2] Furthermore, the Secretary-General stated in this report that:

> The crisis has begun to make deep inroads into the economies of the entire continent. Gross output of developing Africa declined by 0.1 per cent in 1983 and only a marginal growth of 1.8 per cent is projected for 1984. As a result, per capita income has consistently declined since 1980 at an average annual rate of 4.1 per cent[...]. In 1983, although the terms of trade have somewhat improved, the quantity of export has shown the largest annual decrease since 1974. By 1983, external debt amounted to $150 billion, of which $120 billion were disbursed, with servicing cost amounting to 22.4 per cent of total earnings. Other factors are deteriorating terms of trade, a rise in interest rates, and a decline in real terms of concessional financing. Net disbursements of official development assistance (ODA) for sub-Saharan Africa declined from $8.3 billion to $8 billion in 1982. (UN document No. A/39/594 of 23 October 1984, parag. 5)

As Edgar Pisani, the Chairman of the Preparatory Committee for the 13th Special Session, notes in his statement: "While there [were] differences of interpretation concerning the causes of the present situation in Africa, there [was] a consensus on the characteristics of that situation."[3] In this sense, the majority of the member states of the UN,[4] and many outside observers (World Bank, 1981, 1984; Ravenhill, J., Ed., 1986, among others), agreed that the critical economic and social conditions of Africa at the beginning of the 1980s were mainly characterized by:

- Falling per capita GNP,[5]
- Falling per capita food production,[6]
- Very high population growth rate,[7]
- Increasing external debt,[8]
- Declining international assistance,[9] and
- Severe environmental degradation and drought, causing famine and hunger in many countries.[10]

Following the above report of the UN Secretary-General[11] and a request made by the UN Economic and Social Council (ECOSOC),[12] the UN General Assembly decided to include in the agenda of its 39th Ordinary Session of 1984 an item entitled "Critical economic situation in Africa." The debate on this item resulted in the adoption of resolution 39/29 of December 3, 1984, the annex to which contained the "Declaration on the Critical Economic Situation in Africa."[13] By adopting this resolution, the UN officially recognized that the economic situation in Africa was indeed critical, and required a "concerted action by the international community to assist the efforts of the African governments by providing immediate emergency relief, and medium and long-term development aid."[14]

Despite this "concerted action," the situation continued to deteriorate in most African countries in 1985. Consequently, the Assembly of Heads of State and Government of the Organization of African Unity (OAU), held in Addis Ababa, in July 1985, called for a Special Session of the UN General Assembly to deal with this critical economic and social situation.[15] In response to this call, the UN General Assembly took another step forward by adopting resolution 40/40 of December 2, 1985, by which it decided to "convene a special session of the General Assembly at the ministerial level to consider in depth the critical economic situation in Africa."[16] Ultimately, it was during this 13th Special Session that Resolution S-13/2 of June 1st, 1986 and its annex containing UNPAAERD[17] was adopted.

In explaining the causes of the critical economic and social conditions in the 1980s, Resolution S-13/2, annex I, underscored the existence of *initial* or *structural conditions*, which were also described in some parts of the resolution as a "persistent economic crisis," and in other parts as "structural economic problems." In line with this explanation, Resolution S-13/2, annex I, stated that:

> The *persistent economic crisis* in Africa has been aggravated by a combination of *exogenous* and *endogenous factors*. The *endogenous aggravating factors* include deficiencies in institutional and physical infrastructures, economic strategies and policies that have fallen short, in some cases, of achieving their objectives, disparities in urban and rural development and income distribution, insufficient managerial/ administrative capacities, inadequate human resource development, and lack of financial resources, the demographic factors and political instability manifested, *inter alia,* in a large and growing population of refugees [...]. The *serious aggravating exogenous factors* include the

recent international economic recession, the decline in commodity prices, adverse terms of trade, the decline in financial flows, increased protectionism and high interest rates. The heavy burden of debt and debt-servicing obligations also constrains Africa's prospects for economic growth. (UN document No. A/RES/S-13/2 of 01 June 1985, annex I, parag. 3) (Emphasis added)

This is the interpretation that came out of the formal and informal consultations conducted by the Preparatory Committee and the Ad Hoc Committee in charge of drafting Resolution S-13/2 and its annex.[18] It is in this sense that we describe this interpretation as the "consensual interpretation" of the causes of the critical economic and social conditions in Africa in the 1980s.[19]

This "consensual interpretation" is, however, inconsistent with the measures adopted under UNPAAERD. To begin with, the authors of Resolution S-13/2 did not define what they precisely meant by "persistent economic crisis" or "structural economic problem."[20] Furthermore, they did not clearly indicate whether the initial conditions or the internal and external aggravating factors were the most important problems to be solved immediately. Moreover, they did not explain how and why the development of agriculture and the sectors in support of agriculture prescribed in UNPAAERD would solve any of these problems. In sum, the "consensual interpretation" provided by Resolution S-13/2, annex I, would not be very useful for any policy maker to formulate an effective development program.

During the 13th Special Session of the UN General Assembly, two groups of countries dominated and ultimately shaped the formulation and implementation of UNPAAERD. These two influential groups were: (1) the group of African countries, which was supported by the Group of 77[21] and the group of Non-Aligned countries,[22] and (2) the group of capitalist developed countries, which was backed by the two powerful Bretton Woods institutions (i.e., the World Bank and the International Monetary Fund). By the mid-1980s, the group of socialist countries was losing their influence within the UN General Assembly. In fact, no other group endorsed the position of the traditional leader of this group (i.e., the Soviet Union), which interpreted the critical economic and social conditions in Africa as the result of the past colonial exploitation of Africa by the European countries.[23] Consequently, in the following discussions, we will focus on the proposals submitted by the group of African countries and the group of capitalist developed countries.

Table 2.1 – The Different Interpretations of the Causes of the Critical Economic and Social Conditions in Africa in the 1980s

	The "Consensual Interpretation," according to Resolution S-13/2	African Countries' Interpretation	Capitalist Developed Countries' Interpretation
Causes	Persistent economic crisis and/or structural economic problems AGGRAVATED BY: 1) *Endogenous factors,* including deficiencies in institutional and physical infrastructures, inadequate economic strategies and policies, insufficient managerial/administrative capacities, inadequate human resource development, lack of financial resources, and 2) *Exogenous factors,* including international economic recession, decline in commodity prices, adverse terms of trade, decline in financial flows, increased protectionism and high interest rates, heavy burden of debt and debt-servicing obligations, etc.	Lack of structural transformation (i.e., lack of industrialization), and lack of diversification of the African economies LED TO: 1) Dependence of the African economies on the export of narrow range of primary commodities on the international trade, and 2) Vulnerability of the African economies to external shocks.	Economic mismanagement, adoption of inadequate economic policies, and inadequate political and economic institutions by African governments LED TO: 1) Imbalances of internal and external accounts, 2) Lack of incentive to produce, 3) Declining production, 4) Debt crisis, etc.
Consequences	Critical economic and social conditions in Africa in the 1980s	Critical economic and social conditions in Africa in the 1980s	Critical economic and social conditions in Africa in the 1980s

In its submission to the 13th Special Session of the UN General Assembly,[24] the group of African countries explained the causes of the critical economic and social conditionals in Africa in the 1980s as follows:

> The African economic crisis is due principally to *insufficient structural transformation* and the *economic diversification* that are required to move the continent away from inherited colonial economic structures, typified by a vicious interaction between excruciating poverty and abysmally low levels of productivity, in an environment marked by serious deficiencies in basic economic and social infrastructures, most especially the physical capital, research capabilities, technological know-how and human resources development that are indispensable to an integrated and dynamic economy. (UN document No. A/AC/.229/2 of 23 April 1986, p. 7, parag. 14) (Emphasis added)

The group of African countries also argued that the lack of structural transformation and diversification of the African economies was the origin of their *dependence* on the "export of narrow range of primary commodities" in its international trade.[25] Moreover, the group argued that the situation of dependence combined with other factors (particularly the weak linkages among the economic and social sectors, and the existence of socio-economic dualism) led to the vulnerability of the African economies to external shocks and, ultimately, to the critical economic and social situation of the 1980s.[26]

In order to understand this African interpretation, we need to know that it was based on a development program entitled *Africa's Priority Programme for Economic Recovery 1986-1990 (APPER)*, which was adopted by the Organisation of African Unity (OAU) in July 1985. And this program was itself "firmly rooted" in the *Lagos Plan of Action for the Implementation of the Monrovia Strategy for the Economic Development of Africa*,[27] simply known as the *Lagos Plan of Action (LPA)*, adopted by the OAU in April 1980.[28]

In the same way as the *LPA*, *APPER* was based on the strategy of "collective self-reliance" of the OAU. However, while the *LPA* was designed to deal with the long-term objectives of "structural transformation" (i.e., industrialization) of the African economies, the *APPER* was formulated to address the short-term problems of declining agricultural and food production in Africa in the 1980s.[29] In connection with this, the OAU justified the *APPER*'s focus on agricultural development with the two following reasons: (1) the agricultural sector was very important for the African economies, since it provided the "livelihood for close to 80 per cent of the African population";[30] and (2) the OAU needed to "ensure that African countries [would] never again have to go through the disastrous and humiliating consequences of famine."[31] In addition to these two reasons, the literature on structuralist theory and dependency theory of development[32] suggests that most developing countries which have adopted development strategies or programs based on these theories tend to use the revenue squeezed from the agricultural sector to finance their industrialization (Rapley, 1996: 29).

By the mid-1980s, the explanation of the African economic and social problems by the capitalist developed countries – in collaboration with the World Bank and the IMF – and the solutions they commonly proposed, were well-known. These solutions, generally described as *structural adjustment programs* (SAPs), have been already applied in at least 29 African countries by the end of the 1980s (World Bank, 1994b). These SAPs may have taken different forms, depending on the period and the country where they were applied. However, despite their different forms, the SAPs consisted of economic and political reforms administered jointly by the IMF and the World Bank, and supported by the capitalist developed countries, particularly the United States. Describing the recent forms of SAPs, Lionel Demery notes that:

> In its newer theoretical and institutional form, structural adjustment rests on three main components: the importance of *macroeconomic stability;* the need for *prices to* reflect relative scarcities; and a reduction in the *role of the state* in directing and administering economic activity. Each of these components of structural adjustment interacts with the others, and the distinction between them should not be taken too far. (Demery, 1994: 30)

In order to understand how the group of developed countries interpreted the causes of the African economic and social problems of the 1980s, we need to refer to the analysis of the World Bank (1981, 1984, 1989, 1994). In general, the World Bank recognized the constraints imposed on the African economies by, on the one hand, a set of *internal factors* that "evolved from historical circumstances or from the physical environment" (including underdevelopment of human resources, and rapidly growing population) (World Bank, 1981: 4); and, on the other hand, a *"set of external factors"* (including stagflation in the industrialized countries, higher energy prices, and adverse terms of trade) (World Bank, 1981: 4). However, the World Bank consistently argued that the *internal factors* constituted the major obstacles to the development of African countries, and that the *external factors* could be surmounted by those countries, in the same way as the other developing countries in Latin America and Asia did (World Bank, 1994b). In this sense, the World Bank defined the African economic and social problems of the 1980s as follows:

> There is no single explanation for Africa's poor performance before the adjustment period. The main factors behind the stagnation and decline were poor policies – both macroeconomic and sectorial – emanating from a development paradigm that gave the state a prominent role in production and in regulating economic activity. Overvalued exchange rates and large and prolonged budget deficits undermined the macroeconomic stability needed for long-term growth. Protectionist trade policies and government monopolies reduced the competition so vital for increasing productivity. In addition, the state increased its presence in the 1970s, nationalizing enterprises and financial institutions and introducing a web of regulations and licenses for most economic activities. More important, the development strategy had a clear bias against exports, heavily taxing agricultural exports, one of the largest suppliers of foreign exchange. (World Bank, 1994: 20)

It was in connection with this kind of interpretation that George Schultz, who represented the United States during the 13th Special Session of the UN General Assembly, emphasized in his address the need to "expand the individual human opportunity," the need to shift the international assistance from public to private entities, and the imperative to create an "environment of confidence" through economic and political stabilization.[33] In the same vein, the representative of Netherlands, who spoke on behalf of the European Community emphasized the need to encourage liberal access for trade, the necessity to adopt appropriate environmental and population policies, and the need to tie international assistance with the adoption of structural adjustment programs (SAP).[34] Some of these solutions were included in the APPER and UNPAAERD under the sub-heading "Policy reforms."[35] However, as we will see, they were not the main focus of UNPAAERD.

In taking into consideration the interpretation provided by the World Bank and the proposals made by capitalist developed countries, it can be argued that the group of capitalist developed countries defined the African economic and social problems of the 1980s, not only in terms of economic mismanagement and inadequate economic policies, but also in terms of inadequate political and economic institutions.[36] In this sense, most representatives of developed countries who intervened during the 13th Special Session of the UN General Assembly made it clear that the only valid model of economic development was the capitalist liberal model, based on a competitive market economy. We need to specify, however, that by the mid-1980s, the developed countries did not yet insist on the adoption of democratic and liberal institutions as a solution to the African economic and social problems. This would change by the end of the 1980s and at the beginning of the 1990s, when they would require good governance and democratic institutions as conditions for their support to African countries.

In sum, conflicting interpretations of the causes of the critical economic and social conditions in Africa emerged during the 13th Special Session of the UN General Assembly. While the group of African countries conceived the problems in terms of lack of structural transformation (i.e., lack of industrialization), which would have led to the dependence and vulnerability of African economics, the group of capitalist developed countries pointed out the mismanagement of the African economies and the adoption of inadequate economic policies, and inadequate political and economic institutions by the African political leaders, as the most important causes of the African economic and social problems in the 1980s. However, no matter how the causes of these African economic and social problems were interpreted, the most important policy measures adopted under UNPAAERD were, in fact, drawn from *Africa's Priority Programme for Economic Recovery 1986-1990 (APPER)*.

The Formulation of UNPAAERD

In addressing the question of how UNPAAERD was formulated, we need to analyze the forecasts made by the relevant policy makers and/or stakeholders concerning to the following items:

1. The consequences of existing development programs in Africa, which would justify their replacement by UN-PAAERD,
2. The expected consequences (i.e., goals and objectives) of UNPAAERD,
3. The measures to be included in UNPAAERD, and

4.   The expected behavior of stakeholders (i.e., possible support or opposition to the implementation of the new program).

As in the previous section, we will focus here on the discourses and proposals made by the two most influential groups of policy makers and/or stakeholders within the UN General Assembly: the African group and the group of capitalist developed countries, along with the Bretton Woods Institutions.

1.   Forecasts concerning the consequences of existing development programs in Africa:

The widespread critical economic and social conditions in the 1980s seem to indicate that the adoption of either a capitalist or a socialist model of development by any given African country would not have made any difference. Indeed, capitalist-oriented countries, like Senegal and Côte d' Ivoire, seemed to have similar economic and social problems as the socialist-oriented countries, like Tanzania and Madagascar.

In reality, as a growing number of African countries (capitalist-oriented as well as socialist-oriented countries) were implementing structural adjustment programs (SAPs) since the end of the 1970s, it was the effective implementation of these programs that made the biggest difference between African countries. In this sense, following the classification established by the World Bank (1994b), we will distinguish two groups of African countries, based on the adoption or non-adoption of SAPs: (1) the so-called group of "adjusting countries," which had "reasonable social stability and adjustment programs" and included twenty-nine countries in the second half of the 1980s ;[37] and (2) the so-called "non-adjusting countries," which included nineteen other African countries.[38]

Despite the fact that the majority of African countries were implementing various kinds of SAPs, the OAU and the UN Economic Commission for Africa (UNECA or ECA) were strongly opposed to these programs. The main reason for this opposition was the high political and social costs of the programs, which were generally associated with unpopular measures such as cuts in social programs, higher unemployment rates due to the closing of inefficient public enterprises, higher food prices, etc. (Ravenhill, J.: 1986a: 5). Consequently, in its forecast about the consequences of the existing development programs, the group of African countries argued that, at best, the SAPs did not make any difference and, at worst, they have aggravated the critical economic and social conditions in Africa. In line with this argument, the ECA, which usually spoke for Africa, projected that:

> The picture that emerges from the analysis of the perspective of the African region by the year 2008 under the historical trend scenario is almost a nightmare. Poverty would reach unimaginable dimensions since rural incomes would become almost negligible relative to the cost of the physical goods and services. The conditions in the urban centres also worsen with more shanty towns, more congested roads, more beggars and more delinquents. The level of unemployed searching desperately for the means to survive imply increased crimes rates and misery. Against such a background of misery and social injustice, the political situation would inevitably be difficult. (UNECA, 1983: 93-94, quoted in Ravenhill, J. 1986a: 1).

It was on the basis of such bleak projection that the group of African countries was looking for an alternative to the existing development programs in Africa, including the SAPs.

For its part, the group of capitalist developed countries, along with the IMF and the World Bank, continued to support the SAPs, and began to tie the disbursement of official development assistance (ODA) and debt arrangement (cancellation or reduction of official debt) with the adoption of SAPs by individual African governments. In their forecasts about the consequences of the SAPs, the capitalist developed countries clearly indicated that the adoption of these programs was the only way to solve the economic and social problems in Africa, and their rejection meant further deterioration of the economic and social conditions. In connection with these forecasts, George Shultz, in his address to the 13th Special Session of the UN General Assembly, was very confident with regard to the positive results of SAPs, and suggested to increase the role of the IMF and the World Bank.[39] The representative of Netherlands, who spoke on behalf of the European Community, welcomed the growing number of African countries undertaking SAPs, and also declared the support of the European Community for an increasing role for the IMF and the World Bank in African development.[40]

In sum, there was an important divergence of views between the group of African countries and that of the capitalist developed countries with regard to the consequences of the SAPs. However, despite the capitalist developed countries' argument about the positive effects of the SAPs, the African argument against these programs prevailed during the 13ᵗʰ Special Session of the UN General Assembly and strongly influenced the formulation of UNPAAERD. In this sense, UNPAAERD was designed to replace the SAPs sponsored by the capitalist developed countries with the Bretton Woods institutions.

2. *Forecasts concerning the expected consequences of UNPAAERD:*

Before discussing the expected consequences (i.e., goals and objectives) of UNPAAERD, it is worth noting that Resolution S-13/2 and most UN documents did not make any difference between *policy goals* and *policy objectives*, as some policy analysts like William Dunn (1994) would suggest.[41] Thus, concerning the expected consequences of UNPAAERD, instead of defining specific objectives, Resolution S-13/2 gave a list of goals, which included the achievement of "sustained economic and social development,"[42] the paving of "the way for self-reliant economic development,"[43] and the launching of the African continent on "the path of dynamic self-reliant and self-sustained economic development in a favourable external environment."[44]

Abdou Diouf, former President of Senegal and former Chairman of the OAU, who spoke on behalf of the group of African countries during the 13ᵗʰ Special Session of the UN General Assembly, summarized the expectation of this group as follows:

> [UNPAAERD] should make it possible for Africa to attain *food self-reliance* and the objective of *economic growth* and *self-focused and self-sustained development* at the national, regional and international level. (Official Records of the UN General Assembly, Thirteen Special Session, 1st Plenary Meeting, UN document No. A/S-13/PV.1-8, p. 6) (Emphasis added)

However, while agreeing with the goal of achieving *food self-reliance*, the capitalist developed countries generally viewed the *economic development* of Africa as the most important outcome expected from the new program. In connection with this, George Shultz talked about a "successful economic development" based on the "expansion of individual human opportunity."[45] He stated that, in order to achieve this, the "development experience [of the United States] is a useful guide to productive economic policies."[46]

Some policy analysts (particularly Dunn, 1994; and Jones, 1977) argued that, in order to ensure the effectiveness of any public policy, its goals and objectives have to be clearly and realistically defined. Thus, given the vague definition of the goals and objectives of UNPAAERD in Resolution S-13/2, this development program was unlikely to be effective from the beginning.

3. Forecasts concerning the measures to be included in UNPAAERD:

With regard to the measures to be included in UNPAAERD, in application of resolution 40/40 of 15 January 1986, convening the 13th Special Session of the UN General Assembly, it was understood that the Preparatory Committee, the Ad Hoc Committee and the General Assembly would receive the proposals submitted by the Secretary General and other bodies of the UN, and member states. However, it was also made clear that these entities should take "fully into account the priorities set by the Assembly of Heads of State and Government of the Organisation of African Unity."[47] Accordingly, in application of this disposition, the Chairman of the Preparatory Committee simply suggested that the APPER "furnish the basis for discussion in determining the action to be taken."[48]

Thus, following the priorities set by the OAU, the measures related to the *development of agriculture and the other sectors in support of agriculture* contained in the APPER became the most important measures included in UNPAAERD.[49] As Abdou Diouf put it: "agriculture is the core of the all our work and the corner-stone of the entire conceptual edifice proposed for the [UN General] Assembly's consideration."[50] In fact, as mentioned earlier, the OAU justified the APPER's focus on agriculture by the importance of the agricultural sector in African economies, and by the recurrence of hunger and famine in many African countries during the 1980s.

In addition to the measures related to the development of agriculture and other sectors in support of agriculture, the other measures contained in UNPAAERD include:

- Fight against drought and desertification,
- Human resources development,
- Policy reforms (particularly macroeconomic adjustments, population policy, popular participation and integration of women in the process of development),

- South-South cooperation, and
- International financial support.[51]

The inclusion of measures related to the SAPs, described in UNPAAERD as *"policy reforms,"* can be explained by the fact that the majority of the African countries were already implementing these measures. However, according to some analysts, these measures were adopted by the OAU and most African countries, along with the acceptance of their responsibilities in the critical economic and social situation of the 1980s, just to accommodate the capitalist developed countries and to get the much needed financial support from them (Mongula, 1994).

While most of the other capitalist developed countries expressed their agreement with regard to the contents of UNPAAERD, the United States openly opposed the priorities set in this program, and made a reservation about these priorities. Indeed, the representative of the United States during the last meeting of the 13th Special Session stated that for his country, "economic restructuring" is the number-one priority for Africa. Nothing short of this will spark renewed growth."[52] In addition to the SAPs, the other important elements to be included in the new program, according to the United States, would be agricultural growth, human resources development, and famine preparation.[53]

In sum, with regard to its contents, UNPAAERD was mainly based on the priorities set by the OAU in the APPER, which focused on the development of both the agriculture and the sectors in support of agriculture. Other measures related to the SAPs were also included in UNPAAERD. But these measures were secondary, and might have been integrated just by political expediency. In addition, the reservation made by the United States concerning these priorities foreshadowed some problems related to the implementation of this program. We will discuss in depth these problems of implementation in the following sections.

4. Forecasts concerning the expected behavior of the international community:

Concerning the expected behavior of the international community vis-à-vis UNPAAERD, the group of African countries was very optimistic. It forecasted strong support for the implementation of the new program from the whole international community. Indeed, speaking on behalf on the OAU, Abdou Diouf expressed his hope that UNPAAERD would be "accepted as the *general framework* for assistance by the international community to Africa."[54]

However, despite the fact that most capitalist developed countries did not openly reject the new program, some members of this groups indicated that they would not totally comply with the measures contained in UNPAAERD. In connection with this, as mentioned earlier, the United States made it clear that it would not consider UNPAAERD's focus on agricultural development as the number-one priority for Africa. Instead, it would strongly support "the bold steps for policy reform called for in the Programme."[55] In addition, the United States also indicated that it would pursue its own development programs with individual African countries. Particularly, it would pursue its "Economic Policy Reform Program," and would continue to support the SAPs sponsored by the World Bank/ IMF.

For its part, the European Community agreed with UNPAAERD's focus on agricultural development, but indicated that it would focus on small holders. In addition, it would also continue to support the World Bank and IMF sponsored SAPs, and would tie the international assistance to African countries with the adoption of SAPs by the recipient country.[56]

In sum, while the African countries expected strong support for the implementation of UNPAAERD from all members of the international community, the capitalist developed countries, which controlled the bulk of the much needed financial resources necessary for its implementation, generally insisted on the continuation of the SAPs.

The Adoption of UNPAAERD

In addressing the question of how UNPAAERD was adopted by the UN General Assembly, we need to analyze Resolution S-13/2 and discuss the criteria that have been taken into consideration in the process of recommendation.

The Preparatory Committee, established by resolution 40/40 of 15 January 1986, which convened the 13th Special Session of the UN General Assembly, played important roles in drafting and recommending UNPAAERD. This Preparatory Committee and the Ad Hoc Committee created during the Special Session were mandated to undertake "the necessary preparations to ensure the success of the [13th special] session."[57] In connection with this, as mentioned earlier, it was entrusted to receive proposals from the UN bodies and member states, and particularly to take "fully into account" the priorities set by the OAU in the APPER.[58]

The Preparatory Committee, chaired by Edgar Pisani of France, held formal and informal meetings, between January 23 and May 23, 1986, and received the following documents:

- Memorandum transmitted by the government of Morocco,[59]
- Africa's submission to the Special Session of the United Nations General Assembly on Africa's Economic and Social Crisis,"[60] and
- Draft of UNPAAERD, prepared by the group of African countries.[61]

In application of resolution 40/40 which recommended that the priorities set by the African countries should be taken fully into consideration, the Preparatory Committee decided to include the APPER as part of the draft resolution containing UNPAARED. As a result, Resolution S-13/2 which contained UNPAAERD was, in reality, the UN resolution for the implementation of the APPER.

In order to pursue the work of the Preparatory Committee of the 13th Special Session, an Ad Hoc Committee was created. This Ad Hoc Committee, chaired by Stephen Lewis of Canada, was mandated to receive the proposals submitted by member states, and to prepare the "final document or documents for consideration by the General Assembly."[62] Thus, in addition to the draft of UNPAAERD prepared by the group of African countries,[63] the Ad Hoc Committee also received the following documents:

- Economic Development and the Transformation of African Agriculture, submitted by Israel,[64]
- Economic Assistance of the German Democratic Republic to the African States, submitted by German Democratic Republic,[65]
- Economic Relations of the USSR with the Countries of Africa, submitted by the Union of the Soviet Socialist Republics,[66]
- Economic Assistance Given by Czechoslovakia to African Countries in 1985, submitted by Czechoslovakia,[67]
- Joint Statement of the Group of Socialist Countries,[68] and Amendments to the Draft of UNPAAERD, as Contained in the

UN document No. A/S-13/4, Annex V, submitted by Poland;[69] and

- Draft resolution entitled "1986-1990 Quinquennium for International Economic and Technical Co-operation with Africa," submitted by Mexico.[70]

However, as the report of the Ad Hoc Committee showed, only the draft of UNPAAERD submitted by the Preparatory Committee and the draft resolution from Mexico were taken into consideration by the Ad Hoc Committee. Furthermore, after some discussions within this committee, the Mexican draft resolution itself was withdrawn and replaced by a paragraph to be integrated in the final draft of UNPAAERD. The resilience of the African proposal can be explained by the provisions of resolution 40/40, which stipulates that the priorities set by the OAU should be taken fully into consideration in the formulation of the new development program for Africa.[71] In addition, this resilience can be also explained by the strong influence of the African group, supported by the Group of 77 (G77) and the Non-Aligned Movement, within the UN (Nyangoni, 1985; Wilkins, 1981).

Therefore, if we refer to the different criteria of policy recommendation (effectiveness, efficiency, adequacy, equity, responsiveness, and appropriateness) suggested by policy analysts, such as William Dunn (1994), we can argue that the criterion of *responsiveness*[72] was the only criterion which compelled the Preparatory Committee and the Ad Hoc Committee to recommend the final draft of UNPAAERD to the UN General Assembly for adoption. In other words, UNPAAERD was recommended to the UN General Assembly not because of its potential effectiveness, efficiency, adequacy, equity and appropriateness, but because of its *responsiveness* to the preferences or values of the group of African countries. In connection with this, all other proposals were discarded, not because of their lack of effectiveness, efficiency, adequacy, equity and appropriateness, but because of their lack of *responsiveness* to the needs, preferences, or values of the group of African countries.

Finally, the procedure of "adoption *without vote*," which was applied for the adoption of UNPAAERD, allowed the adoption of UNPAAERD by the UN General Assembly, without any possibility of rejection of this program by any country. Unfortunately, as we will see in the next section, its implementation was mainly hampered by the non-compliance of the member states.

The Implementation and Evaluation of UNPAAERD

In addressing the question of how UNPAAERD was implemented, we need to look at the *policy actions* (i.e., inputs and processes) that took place under this program, and their *consequences* (i.e., outputs and impacts). This analysis will allow us to see whether the African countries and the international community really complied with the provisions of UNPAAERD.

In application of the concept of *global compact*, Resolution S-13/2, annex II, stipulated, on the one hand, that the African countries, were committed to mobilize domestic resources and to implement the measures contained in UNPAAERD;[73] and, it also stipulated, on the other hand, that the international community was committed to support and complement the African development efforts by enhancing the quantity, quality, and modality of official development assistance (ODA), by improving the international economic environment (which would include the elimination of protectionism), and by reducing or canceling the external debt of African countries.[74]

More specifically, in terms of inputs, the group of African countries estimated that the "full implementation" of UNPAAERD would require $128.1 billion during the period 1986-1990.[75] Of this total cost, the African countries would provide $82.5 billion or 64.4 per cent through the mobilization of domestic resources; and the international community would provide $46 billion or 35.6 per cent, mainly through the increase of ODA and debt reduction. Thus, according to the estimates of the policy makers, the additional contribution of each entity for the implementation of UNPAAERD would amount to $16.5 billion a year for the African countries, and $9.2 billion a year for the international community.[76]

However, comparing the financial resources available to the African countries before and after the adoption of UNPAAERD,[77] we found that, during the period of the implementation of UNPAAERD (1986- 1990), most African countries failed to increase the level of their domestic savings and investment. For its part, the international community also failed to provide the additional $9.2 billion a year in ODA, even though it did significantly increase its financial contribution to Africa.

Table 2.2 – Implementation of UNPAAERD:
Available Financial Resources

Available Financial Resources	1980-1985	1986-1990
1 – Domestic Resources		
- Gross domestic savings (annual average as percentage of GDP)	21.5	18.5
- Gross domestic investment (annual average as percentage of GDP)	23.1	20.2
- Gross domestic investment (annual average in billions of dollars, in constant 1987 prices)	86.0	83.5
2 – External Resources		
- Net official development assistance (annual average in billions of dollars, in constant 1987 prices)	12.1	16.2
- Net official development assistance (annual average percentage growth rate, in constant 1987 prices)	-0.1	10.0
- Net foreign direct investment (annual average in billions of dollars, in 1987 prices)	0.6	1.4

Source: World Bank (1995).

Table 2.3 - Implementation of UNPAAERD:
Economic and social conditions in Africa in 1986-1990

Economic and social Development Indicators	1980-1985	1986-1990
1 - Economic Growth		
- Annual average percentage growth rate of GDP	1.7	1.7
- Annual average per capita GNP (in US dollars, Atlas method)	761	690
2 – Agricultural Development		
- Value added in agriculture (annual average percentage growth rate)	0.7	1.4
- Food import (annual average percentage growth rate)	0.1	3.3
3 - Industrial development		
- Value added in industry (annual average percentage growth rate)	1.9	0.9
4-) Human resource development		
- Adult literacy (percentage)	44	50
- Life expectancy at birth	50	54
5-) Economic stabilization		
- Budget deficit (as percentage of GDP)	7.2	6.9
- Total external debt (annual average in billions of dollars, current prices)	181	273

Source: World Bank (1995).

Concerning the African domestic financial resources, as a percentage of GDP, the level of gross domestic investment in Africa dropped from an average of 23.1 per cent a year during the period 1980-1985 to an average of 20.2 per cent during the period 1985-1990.[78] In constant 1987 prices, there was respectively a decline from $86 billion a year to $83.5 billion a year. Consequently, there was an important gap between what was expected to be the contribution of African countries for the implementation of UNPAAERD, and what they were able to provide ($83.5 billion a year). As a result, Africa could not carry out its part of the *global compact*, which consisted in providing additional $16.5 billion a year (that is 64.4 per cent of the total cost required for the implementation of UNPAAERD) through mobilization of its domestic resources.

With regard to the external financial resources, the net ODA to Africa increased in current prices, from an average of $10.4 billion a year during the period 1980-1985 to $17 billion a year during the period of 1985-1990. In constant 1987 prices, the increase was respectively from $12.1 billion to $16.2 billion.[79] In terms of annual average percentage growth, there was, in constant 1987 prices, an increase of about 10 per cent a year during the period 1985-1990, against a decline of 0.1 per cent a year during the previous period. In addition to the net ODA, the amount of foreign direct investment (FDI) also increased, in constant 1987 prices, from $0.6 billion a year during the period 1980-1985 to $1.4 billion a year during the period of 1985-1990.[80] However, the additional contribution by the international community during the period of 1985-1990 amounted only to $6.6 billion a year in current prices (or $4.1 billion in constant 1987 prices). In other words, the international community failed to provide the targeted $9.2 billion a year expected by the policy makers. Consequently, both the African countries and the international community failed to carry out their respective part of the *global compact*.

Concerning the policy processes required for the implementation of UNPAAERD, Resolution S-13/2 recommended, on the one hand, that all governments "take effective action for the rapid implementation of the Programme of Action"[81]; and on the other hand, that the organs, organizations and bodies of the United Nations system "participate fully in and support the implementation" of the program.[82] In addition, all intergovernmental and non-governmental organizations were also called "to support and contribute to the implementation of the

Programme of Action."[83]

In fact, there was no specific entity (individual or organization) designated to administer UNPAAERD. The role of the Secretary-General of the UN was indeed limited "to monitor the process of implementation of the Programme of Action and to report thereon to the General Assembly at its forty-second and forty-third sessions."[84] He was not in control of the resources required for the implementation of the program, nor could he obligate member states and international organizations to comply with its prescription. Not surprisingly, the final review of UNPAAERD pointed out this lack of specific program administrator as one of the important causes of its failure. As the final review put it: "The Programme of Action itself was silent regarding who was to act if unforeseen exogenous contingencies threw the Programme of Action off course; also, its review machinery did not clearly address this issue."[85]

Moreover, contrary to the expectation of the African countries that UNPAAERD would become the general framework for assistance by the international community to Africa, most international donors and development agencies – in particular, the Word Bank, the IMF, and even the UNDP – continued to undertake their own development programs with individual African countries.[86] Following the example of the United States, most developed countries did not comply with the priorities set by the African countries in UNPAAERD. They continued to require the adoption of SAPs as a condition for providing increased ODA and debt cancellation or reduction. As a result, the roles of both the World Bank and the IMF in African development increased tremendously during the period of the implementation of UNPAAERD. Particularly, the World Bank sponsored for each African country client a "consultative group of international donors," which became a very important institution, through which individual African countries were granted, among other things, ODA and debt cancellation or reduction. Paradoxically, even the UNDP, which is part of the UN organization, continued to organize its own "round-table discussions" at the level of each individual African country, and did not take any specific action under UNPAAERD.

With regard to the evaluation of UNPAAERD, since the policy actions (i.e., inputs and processes) expected under this program did not come forth, there was logically no consequence to be expected from it. Nonetheless, we need to look at the African economic and social conditions at the end of the implementation of UNPAAERD in order to evaluate whether the objectives of this program have been achieved, regardless of the fact that neither policy inputs nor policy processes have been adequate.

Comparing the economic and social conditions in Africa before and after the adoption of UNPAAERD,[87] we found that the growth rate of the GDP of Africa as a whole, during the implementation of UNPAAERD (1986-1990), remained at the same level (1.7 per cent a year) as the period before. Therefore, as the population growth rate remained also at the high level of 2.8 per cent a year (World Bank, 1995: 7), the per capita GNP steadily declined from an average of $761 in 1980-1985 to $690 in 1986-1990.

Concerning the agricultural development, which was the main focus of UNPAAERD, the annual average percentage growth rate of agricultural production in Africa increased from 0.7 per cent during the period of 1980-1985 to 1.4 per cent during the period of 1985-1990.[88] However, instead of moving toward food self-sufficiency, Africa actually became increasingly dependent on food imports, as they jumped from an annual average percentage growth rate of 0.1 per cent during the period of 1980-1985 to 3.3 per cent during the period of 1986-1990.[89] Consequently, the most important goal of UNPAAERD (food self-sufficiency) was totally missed. In addition, the industrial sector was also declining in Africa, as the percentage growth of the value added in industry decreased from 1.9 per cent a year in 1980-1985 to 0.9 per cent in 1985-1990.[90]

In sum, despite the improvement of some economic and social indicators, particularly in terms of literacy, life expectancy at birth, and budget deficit,[91] UNPAAERD was ineffective in dealing with the major economic and social problems of Africa in the 1980s. Although the UN General Assembly refused to admit the total failure of this program, it did recognize some of its shortcomings in the final review, which stated that:

> none of the goals of the Programme of Action were fully realized. Targets for growth, food security, human investment and debt reduction were missed, so declines rather than hoped-for increases have been recorded by many States and for Africa as a whole. (UN document No. A/RES/46/151 of 18 December 1991, Annex I.A, parag. 9)

Conclusion

UNPAAERD was ineffective in dealing with the critical economic and social conditions in Africa in the 1980s. Most of its goals and objectives were missed, and the economic and social conditions in Africa actually worsened by the end of its period of implementation. The UN General Assembly acknowledged to some extent the failure of UNPAAERD to accomplish its objectives, but it paradoxically argued that:

> [UNPAAERD] was *far from being a failure*. It assisted in focusing the attention of African and other Governments on the basic economic, human and governance problems of Africa. By doing so, it did achieve policy and efficiency gains and averted a more severe decline in net resource inflows. As a result, the economic decline afflicting Africa from 1981 to 1985 was slowed and, in many countries, halted. Furthermore, the process of African policy restructuring and its interaction with the analyses of external partners have led to substantial lessons of experience for all concerned. (UN document No. A/RES/46/151 of 18 December 1991, annex I.A, parag. 12) (Emphasis added)

This statement reveals how inconsistent the UN General Assembly was in evaluating UNPAAERD. In fact, this inadequate evaluation led the UN General Assembly to repeat the same mistakes in the formulation and implementation of the second UN development program for Africa, the United Nations New Agenda or the Development of Africa in the 1990s (UNNADAF).

Notes

[1] Resolution S-13/2 of 1 June 1986, UN document No. A/RES/S-13/2, the annex to which contains the United Nations Programme of Action for the African Economic Recovery and Development 1986-1990 (UNPAAERD).

[2] UN document No. A/39/594 of 23 October 1984, parag. 2.

[3] UN document No. A/S-13/4 of 23 May 1986, annex I, p. 11.

[4] It is obvious that states or countries do not act, but their representatives do on behalf of their respective state or country. In connection with this, we will adopt the convention established within the UN, according to which it is the state or country itself which is virtually acting through its representatives.

[5] According to the World Bank (1993), the per capita gross national product (GNP) for sub-Saharan Africa fell from $570 in 1980 to $490 in 1985, that is a decline of 3.1 per cent a year (World Bank, 1993: 2- 3).

[6] According to J. Ravenhill, "per capita food production fell by 2 per cent a year in the period 1980-1984" (Ravenhill, J. Ed. 1986: ix).

[7] According to the World Bank (1995), the average annual growth rate of the population during the period 1980-1985 was 2.9 per cent for all Africa, and 3.0 for sub-Saharan Africa.

[8] According to the World Bank, the total external debt of all Africa increased, in current price, from $111.6 billion in 1980 to $181.4 billion in 1985.

[9] According to the World Bank (1995), the net official development assistance (ODA) to Africa increased in current prices by 3.8 per cent a year during the period 1980-1985. However, in real terms, there was a slight decline according to the report of the Secretary-General (UN document No. A/39/594 of 23 October 1984, parag. 5).

[10] See the above report of the UN Secretary-General (UN document No. A/39/594 of 23 October 1984).

[11] UN document No. A/39/594 of 23 October 1984.

[12] UN document No. E/1984/188 of 27 July 1984.

[13] UN document No. A/RES/39/29 of 03 December 1984, annex.

[14] *Ibid.*, preamble.

[15] UN document No. 40/666, annex I, declaration AHG/Decl.1(XXI), annex.

[16] UN document No. 40/40 of 02 December 1985, parag. 2.

[17] See Appendix A, below.

[18] See Official Records of 13th Special Session of the UN General Assembly, Summary Record of the Meetings of the Ad Hoc Committee, UN document No. A/S-13/AC.1/SR.1-3, 29 May-3 June 1986.

[19] See Table 2.1 – The Different Interpretations of the Causes of the Critical Economic and Social Conditions in Africa in the 1980s, below, p. 15.

[20] In Africa's Submission to the Special Session of the UN General Assembly (UN document No. A/AC/.229/2* of 23 April 1986, part I.1.), the two phrases were, in fact, used interchangeably.

[21] The Group of 77 or G-77 is "a coalition of the [developing] countries, formed during the 1964 United Nations Conference on Trade and Development (UNCTAD) in Geneva. Originally composed of 77 states, the coalition now numbers over 120 developing countries and continues to press for concessions from the wealthy states" (Kegley and Wittkopf, 1997: 533).

[22] The organization of Non-Aligned countries, also known as the Non-Aligned Movement (NAM), was "founded in Belgrade in 1961 to promote nonalignment and a reduction of the East-West tension" (Kegley and Wittkopf, 1997: 606).

[23] In his address to the 13th special session of the UN General Assembly, Mr. Vorontsov (Union of Soviet Socialist Republics) stated that the "real causes" of

the economic and social problems of Africa in the 1980s were "rooted in the ills inherited from colonialism, and in the merciless plunder and selfish policies pursued by former colonial Powers towards the African countries." Consequently, he suggested that the capitalist developed countries would have to compensate the African countries for the damage they caused to the economic and social development of these countries (Official Records of the General Assembly, Thirteen Special Session, 2nd Plenary Meeting, UN document No. A/S-13/PV.1-8, p. 29).

[24] UN document No. A/AC/.229/2* of 23 April 1986.

[25] UN document No. A/AC/.229/2* of 23 April 1986, p. 7, parag. 15. It is worth noting that, as used by the African policy makers, the phrase "structural transformation" mainly means industrialization or development of the industrial sector.

[26] See Table 2.1 – The Different Interpretations of the Causes of the Critical Economic and Social Conditions in Africa in the 1980s, above, p. 15.

[27] This is clearly stated in Africa's Submission to the 13th Special Session of the UN General Assembly, UN document No. A/AC.229/2* of 23 April 1986, p. 30, parag. 63.

[28] The *Lagos Plan of Action* is contained in UN document No. A/S-11/14 of 21 August 1980, annex I.

[29] UN document No. A/AC.229/2* of 23 April 1986, p. 4, parag. 4 and 5.

[30] UN document No. A/AC.229/2* of 23 April 1986, p. 30, parag. 65.

[31] *Ibid.*.

[32] Structuralist theory of development was initially developed by such analysts as Raul Prebish (1950), and Hans Singer (1950). Dependency theory, as Rapley (1996: 17) puts it, was a "second generation of structuralism," developed by such analysts as Andre Gunder Frank (1967) and Samir Amin (1967), and Fernando Cardoso and Enzo Faletto (1979). Dependency theory was formulated in reaction against the old structuralism, which favored official development assistance and foreign direct investment, and against modernization theory (Apter, 1965), which was based on the guiding role of the so-called "Westernized elites." The major solution suggested by dependency theorists is, therefore, "autonomous national-development strategies," which require the developing countries to "sever their ties to the world economy and [to] become more self-sufficient" (Rapley, 1996: 18-20).

[33] Address by Mr. Schultz (United States), Official Records of the General Assembly, Thirteen Special Session, 3rd Plenary Meeting, UN document No. A/S-13/PV.1-8, p. 64-66.

[34] Address by Mrs. Schoo (Netherlands), Official Records of the General Assembly, Thirteen Special Session, 1st Plenary Meeting, UN document No. A/S-13/PV.1-8, p. 14.

[35] UN document No. A/RES/S-13/2, annex II.A.1.e.

[36] See Table 2.1 – The Different Interpretations of the Causes of the Critical Economic and Social Conditions in Africa in the 1980s, above, p. 15.

[37] This countries were: Benin, Burkina Faso, Burundi, Cameroon, Central African Republic, Chad, Congo, Comoros, Cote d' Ivoire, Gabon, Gambia, Ghana, Guinea, Guinea-Bissau, Kenya, Madagascar, Malawi, Mali, Mauritania, Mozambique, Niger, Nigeria, Rwanda, Senegal, Sierra Leone, Tanzania, Togo, Uganda, Zambia, and Zimbabwe (World Bank, 1994b).

[38] This group included the following countries: Algeria, Angola, Botswana, Cape Verde, Djibouti, Egypt, Equatorial Guinea, Ethiopia, Lesotho, Liberia, Libya, Mauritius, Morocco, Somalia, Sao Tome and Principe, Seychelles, Sudan, Swaziland, Zaire. Namibia and South Africa were usually excluded from the list of African countries until the mid-1990s. Mauritius was under structural adjustment program at the beginning of the 1980s. It is also included in this list, because it "graduated" from its structural adjustment program by the end of the 1980s (World Bank, 1994b).

[39] Address by Mr. Schultz (United States), Official Records of the General Assembly, Thirteen Special Session, 3rd Plenary Meeting, UN document No. A/S-13/PV.1-8, p. 64-66.

[40] Address by Mrs. Schoo (Netherlands), Official Records of the General Assembly, Thirteen Special Session, 1st Plenary Meeting, UN document No. A/S-13/PV.1 8, p. 15.

[41] According to policy analysts such as William Dunn (1994), the main difference between *goals* and *objectives* is that, in general, goals express broad purposes without quantifying them, while objectives set forth specific and quantifiable aims.

[42] UN document No. A/RES/S-13/2, annex I, parag. 1.

[43] UN document No. A/RES/S-13/2, annex I, parag. 2.

[44] UN document No. A/RES/S-13/2, annex I, parag. 4.

[45] Address by Mr. Schultz (United States), Official Records of the General Assembly, Thirteen Special Session, 3rd Plenary Meeting, UN document No. A/S-13/PV.1-8, p. 64.

[46] *Ibid.*.

[47] UN document No. A/RES/40/40 of 15 January 1986, parag. 6.

[48] UN document No. A/S-13/4* of 23 May 1986, annex I, p. 11.

[49] UN document No. A/RES/S-13/2 of 1 June 1986, annex II.A.1(a) and (b).

[50] Address by Mr. Abdou Diouf (President of the Republic of Senegal and Chairman of the OAU), Official Records of the General Assembly, Thirteen Special Session, 1st Plenary Meeting, UN document No. A/S-13/PV.1-8, p. 6.

[51] UN document No. A/RES/S-13/2 of 1 June 1986, annex II.A.1(c), (d), (e); and annex II.B.

[52] Address by Mr. McPherson (United States), Official Records of the General Assembly, Thirteen Special Session, 8th Plenary Meeting, UN document No. A/S-13/PV.1-8, p. 160.

---

[53] *Ibid..*

[54]   Address by Mr. Abdou Diouf (President of the Republic of Senegal and Chairman of the OAU), Official Records of the General Assembly, Thirteen Special Session, 1st Plenary Meeting, UN document No. A/S-13/PV.1-8, p. 7. (Emphasis added)

[55]   Address by Mr. McPherson, (United States), Official Records of the General Assembly, Thirteen Special Session, 8th Plenary Meeting, UN document No. A/S-13/PV.1-8, p. 160.

[56]   Address by Mrs. Schoo (Netherlands), Official Records of the General Assembly, Thirteen Special Session, 1st Plenary Meeting, UN document No. A/S-13/PV.1-8, pp. 14-16.

[57]   UN document No. A/RES/40/40 of 2 December 1985, parag. 4.

[58]   UN document No. A/RES/40/40 of 2 December 1985, parag. 6.

[59]   UN document No. A/AC.229/3.

[60]   UN document No. A/AC.229/2.

[61]   This draft was later integrated in the final report of the Preparatory Committee. See UN document No. A/S-13/4 of 23 May 1986, annex V.

[62]   UN document No. A/S-13/4 of 23 May 1986, p. 10, parag. 9.

[63]   Contained in the report of the Preparatory Committee, UN document No. A/S-13/4, annex V.

[64]   UN document No. A/S-13/7 of 26 May 1986.

[65]   UN document No. A/S-13/8 of 27 May 1986.

[66]   UN document No. A/S-13/10 of 27 May 1986.

[67]   UN document No. A/S-13/11 of 28 May 1986.

[68]   UN document No. A/S-13/14 of 30 May 1986.

[69]   UN document No. A/S-13/AC.1/L.1.

[70]   UN document No. A/S-13/AC.1/L.2.

[71]   UN document No. A/RES/40/40 of 2 December 1985, parag. 6.

[72]   *Responsiveness* refers to the extent that a policy satisfies the needs, preferences, or values of particular groups (Dunn, 1994: 288).

[73]   UN document No. A/RES/S-13/2 of 1st June 1986, Annex II.A, parag. 8-11.

[74]   UN document No. A/RES/S-13/2 of 1st June 1986, Annex II.A,parag. 14-17.

[75]   UN document No. A/RES/S-13/2 of 1st June 1986, Annex II.A.4, parag. 12.

[76]   *Ibid..*

[77]   See Table 2.2 - Implementation of UNPAAERD: Available Financial Resources, below, p. 29.

[78]   *Ibid..*

[79]   *Ibid..*

[80]   *Ibid..*

[81]   UN document No. A/RES/S-13/2 of 1st June 1986, parag. 3.

[82]   UN document No. A/RES/S-13/2 of 1st June 1986, parag. 4.

[83]   UN document No. A/RES/S-13/2 of 1st June 1986, parag. 5.

[84]   UN document No. A/RES/S-13/2 of 1st June 1986, parag. 7.

[85] UN document No. A/RES/46/151 of 18 December 1991, annex I.A, parag. 2.

[86] *Ibid..*

[87] See Table 2.3 - Implementation of UNPAAERD: Economic and social conditions in Africa (1986-1990), above, p. 30.

[88] *Ibid..*

[89] *Ibid..*

[90] *Ibid..*

[91] *Ibid..*

Chapter 3

The United Nations New Agenda for the Development of Africa in the 1990s (UNNADAF)

The UN General Assembly adopted the United Nations New Agenda for the Development of Africa in the 1990s (UNNADAF) on December 18, 1991,[1] in replacement of the failed UNPAAERD. As with UNPAAERD, the systematic analysis of this second UN development program will lead us to discuss how it was set on the agenda of the UN General Assembly, and how it was formulated, adopted, implemented and evaluated by policy makers and/or stakeholders within and outside of the UN. In formulating UNNADAF, the UN General Assembly seemed to have learned from the failure of UNPAAERD. However, as we will see, this second program was hampered by almost the same factors that contributed to the failure of UNPAAERD.

UNNADAF and the UN Agenda

In addressing the question of how UNNADAF was set on the UN General Assembly agenda, and how the economic and social problems of Africa at the beginning of the 1990s were defined by the different groups of policy makers and/or stakeholders, we need to analyze Resolution 46/151 and its annex, along with the proposals submitted to the UN General Assembly during its 46th Ordinary Session.

Almost everybody who reviewed and evaluated UNPAAERD agreed that this first UN development program for Africa completely failed to achieve its goals and objectives. Even the OAU, the Economic Commission for Africa (UNECA or ECA), and the UN Secretary-General arrived at the same conclusion in their respective reports on the final review and appraisal of UNPAAERD.[2]   Most importantly, almost everybody also agreed with the UN Secretary-General who reported that the "economic and social conditions [in Africa] actually worsened over the five year period of UNPAAERD."[3] Consequently, despite the progress made by some African countries (World Bank, 1994b), the same critical economic and social conditions, which prevailed in Africa since the end of the 1970s, persisted at the beginning of the 1990s. These critical economic and social conditions had the same characteristics as in the 1980s, and included:

- Falling per capita GNP,[4]
- Falling per capita food production, which led to an increased food dependence,[5]
- High population growth rate, which remained at the same level as during the period of 1980-1985 (i.e., 2.9 per cent a year),
- Increasing external debt,[6] and
- Persisting environmental degradation and drought.[7]

Resolution 46/151 and its annex provided a "consensual inter-pretations" of the causes of the continuing critical economic and social conditions in Africa in the 1990s. However, the analysis of the proposals submitted by the relevant groups of policy makers and/or stakeholders will reveal how each group interpreted differently the causes of these critical economic and social conditions.

In identifying the causes of the critical economic and social conditions in Africa in the 1990s, Resolution 46/151, annex I.A, pointed to the following factors:

- Insufficient economic reform by the African governments: "only two thirds of the countries pursued sustained economic reform " (i.e., structural adjustment programs),[8]
- Inadequate international financial support: "net real resource transfers and debt burden reduction were below expectations,"[9]
- Inadequate domestic resource mobilization and allocation: "a number of African states did not, in fact, fully achieve policy and resource allocation adjustment and transformation,"[10]
- War, drought and collapse of terms of trade,[11] and
- Inadequate debate or dialogue between the UN and member

states.[12]

Resolution 46/151 only enumerated these factors, believed to be the causes of the continuing critical economic and social conditions in Africa.[13] There was no attempt to classify, nor to explain how these factors result in the economic and social conditions at the beginning of the 1990s. In fact, as we will see in the formulation of UNNADAF, this list was hardly consistent with the measures adopted under the new program.

The group of African countries advanced a similar interpretation as in the 1980s. Indeed, in its submission on the final review and appraisal of the implementation of UNPAAERD,[14] the Assembly of Heads of State and Government of the OAU argued that:

> The malaise of the African economies is mainly due to the *lack of structural transformation*. [UNPAAERD] did not address this problem; hence structural impediments continue to hamper Africa's progress. While *internal constraints* did contribute to the lack of improvement in socio-economic performance during the UNPAAERD period, it was the *external constraints*, which constituted the main obstacles to recovery and development. Economic performance and the effort to improve it were seriously undermined by an unfavourable external environment; in particular, unremunerative commodity prices and the declining export earnings, deteriorating terms of trade, a heavy debt and debt-servicing burden; and inadequate resource flows. (UN document No. A/46/387 of 29 August 1991, annex II, parag. 9) (Emphasis added)

Thus, according to this African interpretation, the main cause of the continuing critical economic and social conditions in Africa at the beginning of the 1990s was the *"lack of structural transformation,"* which was aggravated by *"external constraints,"* including unremunerative commodity prices, declining export earnings, deteriorating terms of trade, heavy debt and debt-servicing burden, and inadequate resource flows. The internal constraints were also recognized here, but they were considered as secondary.[15]

In connection with this interpretation, the OAU endorsed the *African Alternative Framework to Structural Adjustment Programmes for Socio-Economic Recovery and Transformation* (AAF-SAP), designed by the UN Economic Commission for Africa (UNECA or ECA).[16] Furthermore, it also adopted several measures, that were closely related to the structuralist theory and/or the dependency theory

**Table 3.1 - The Different Interpretations of the Causes of the
Critical Economic and Social Conditions in Africa in the 1990s**

	The "Consensual Interpretation," according to Resolution 46/151	African Countries' Interpretation	Capitalist Developed Countries' Interpretation
Causes	- Insufficient economic reform by African governments; - Inadequate inter-national financial support; - Inadequate domestic resource mobilization and allocation; - War, drought and collapse of terms of trade; and - Inadequate debate or dialogue between the UN and member states.	Lack of structural transformation AGGRAVATED BY: *External constraints* including, unremunerative commodity prices, declining export earnings, deteriorating terms of trade, heavy debt and debt-servicing burden, and inadequate resource flows.	Lack of good governance, accountability, and democracy.
Conse-quences	Continuing critical economic and social conditions in Africa in the 1990s.	Continuing critical economic and social conditions in Africa in the 1990s.	Continuing critical economic and social conditions in Africa in the 1990s.

of development,[17] which included:

1. The development of import-substituting industrialization (ISI), following the prescriptions of the *AAF-SAP*;
2. The promotion of regional and sub-regional cooperation and integration in Africa, particularly, the establishment of the African Economic Community;
3. The promotion of South-South cooperation; and
4. A vague policy of population control.

Contrary to the 13th Special Session of the UN General Assembly in 1986, which led to the adoption of UNPAAERD, the 46th Ordinary Session in 1991, which led to the adoption of UNNADAF, did not seem to have interested the capitalist developed countries. Indeed, the official records of this 46th Session showed that only the United States intervened to explain its position,[18] and only Norway suggested two amendments to Resolution 46/151 and its annex.[19] This was in sharp contrast with the 13th Special Session, during which most capitalist developed countries explained their position and tried to influence to some extent the formulation of UNPAAERD. Since the two amendments suggested by Norway concerned only some minor changes in the formulation of Resolution 46/151 and its annex,[20] we will focus in the following discussion on the position of the United States.

In his address to the 46th session of the UN General Assembly, the representative of the United States stated that:

> [The United States] wanted [Resolution 46/151] to recognize the link between *improved governance and accountability* and the successful and long-term development. While we do not believe that [UNNADAF] has a specific language on this matter as we would have liked, we feel that the spirit of this approach pervades the document. (UN document No. A/46/PV.77, pp. 21-23) (Emphasis added)

This statement shows that the United States moved beyond the position it adopted during the 13th Special Session of the UN General Assembly. Instead of simply suggesting the improvement of the management of the African economies, and the adoption of adequate economic policies as in the 1980s, it was requiring in 1991 "improved governance and accountability" (which would go along with the adoption of democratic institutions, or the democratization of the political processes). In fact, by the beginning of the 1990s, in addition to the adoption of SAPs, most capitalist developed countries, along with the World Bank and the IMF, required good governance, accountability and democracy, as the major conditions for providing international assistance to African countries and other developing countries (Decalo, 1992).

This new position of the United States and the other capitalist developed countries indicates that they viewed the lack of good governance, accountability and democracy as the main causes of the continuing critical economic and social conditions in Africa at the beginning of the 1990s.[21] The changes of their positions can be explained by the recognized failure of socialism and communism (along with different forms of authoritarianism) to promote development and to provide a viable model of development, and by the collapse of the communist block following the fall of the Berlin Wall in 1989. These phenomena helped strengthen the power and influence of the capitalist developed countries in international affairs, and reinforced the belief that only capitalism and democracy can promote sustainable economic and social development.

In sum, while Resolution 46/151 and its annex identified, among other things, a *lack of economic reform* and an *inadequacy of international support* as the major causes of the continuing critical economic and social conditions in Africa at the beginning of the 1990s, the group of African countries persisted in their belief that these critical conditions were mainly due to the "*lack of structural transformation*" (i.e., lack of industrialization) in Africa. For their part, the United States and most capitalist developed countries, along with the World Bank and IMF, moving beyond their position in the 1980s, identified a *lack of good governance, accountability and democracy* as the main causes of the continuing critical economic and social conditions in most African countries at the beginning of the 1990s.[22] However, despite these different interpretations, the formulation of UNNADAF was still strongly influenced by the group of African countries.

The Formulation of UNNADAF

In addressing the question of how UNNADAF was formulated, we need to analyze the forecasts made by the relevant policy makers and/or stakeholders concerning the following items:

1. The consequences of existing development programs in Africa, which would justify their replacement by UNNADAF,
2. The expected consequences (i.e., goals and objectives) of UNNADAF.
3. The measures to be included in UNNADAF, and
4. The expected behavior of stakeholders (i.e., possible support or opposition to the implementation of the new program).

We will focus once again, in this section, on the forecasts made by the two most influential groups of policy makers and/or stakeholders within the UN (i.e., the group of African countries and the group of capitalist developed countries).

1. Forecasts concerning the consequences of existing development programs in Africa:

The SAPs were the most widely applied development programs in Africa at the end of the 1989 and at the beginning of the 1990s. In connection with this, we will refer to the classification established by the World Bank, used in the previous chapter, and focus on the following groups of African countries: (1) the so-called group of "adjusting countries," which were consistently implementing some form of SAPs, and (2) the so-called group of "non-adjusting countries," which were not implementing any form of SAP at all.[23]

Resolution 46/151, annex I.A, recognized that SAPs had some positive results on most "adjusting countries" which made some progress compared to the non-adjusting countries. Indeed, in explaining the continuing economic decline of Africa as a whole, Resolution 46/151 stated that:

> One of the principal causes of this decline was that only two thirds of the countries pursued sustained economic reform [i.e., structural adjustment programs]. Those that did received increased donor assistance and achieved modest gains in per capita gross domestic product, agricultural production and exports. Other countries continued to decline in these indices, causing negative performance for Africa as a whole. (UN document No. A/RES/46/151 of 18 December 1991, Annex I.A, parag. 10)

Thus, a good number of member states within the UN General Assembly, explicitly acknowledged the positive results of the SAPs, described as "economic reform" in most UN documents.   These positive results were also reported in many publications of the World Bank and the IMF (particularly World Bank, 1994a), and other analysts (Shan, Ed., 1994).

However, despite these positive results, the group of African countries continued to reject the SAPs.   In line with this, the UN Economic Commission for Africa (UNECA or ECA), in its *African Alternative Framework to Structural Adjustment Programmes for Socio- Economic Recovery and Transformation (AAF-SAP)*, claimed that:

> both on theoretical and empirical grounds, the conventional [structural adjustment programs] are inadequate in addressing the real causes of economic, financial and social problems facing African countries which are of a structural nature.   There is therefore an urgent need for an alternative to the current stabilization and adjustment programmes in Africa.   (UN document No. A/44/315 of 21 June 1989, annex, p. 25, parag. 72)

2. Forecasts concerning the expected consequences of UNNADAF:

Resolution 46/151 formulated in many different ways the expected consequences of UNNADAF.   To begin with, it stated that the *"priority objectives"* of the new development program were:

> the *accelerated transformation, integration, diversification and growth of the African economies*, in order to strengthen them within the world economy, reduce their vulnerability to external shocks and increase their dynamism, internalize the process of development and enhance self-reliance. (UN document A/RES/46/151 of 18 December 1991, annex II.A, parag. 6) (Emphasis added)

Along with these *priority objectives*, Resolution 46/151 also specified that a *"desirable objective"* would be to achieve an *"average real growth rate of at least 6 per cent per annum of gross national product* [...], in order for the continent to achieve sustained and sustainable economic growth and equitable development, increase income and eradicate poverty."[24]

Furthermore, Resolution 46/151, annex II.A, mentioned other goals and objectives, which included the achievement of "self-sustaining socio-economic growth and development,"[25] and   "the achievement of human-centered goals by the year 2000 in the areas of life expectancy, integration of women in development, child and maternal mortality, nutrition, health, water and sanitation, basic education and shelter."[26]

In order to understand what the group of African countries really expected from UNNADAF, we need to refer to its submission on the final review and appraisal of the implementation of UNPAAERD. According to this submission, the OAU's primary goals were in fact: "to strengthen [the African economies] within the world economy, reduce their vulnerability to external shocks and increase their dynamism, internalize the process of development and enhance self-reliance."[27] These goals were consistent with the OAU's interpretation of the causes of the critical economic and social conditions in Africa in the 1980s and 1990s. Indeed, as mentioned earlier, the group of African countries believed that the main cause of the continuing critical economic and social conditions in Africa at the beginning of the 1990s was the "lack of structural transformation," which would have led to the dependence of the African economies on the world economy and to their vulnerability to external shocks, including unremunerative commodity prices, declining export earnings, deteriorating terms of trade, etc.

Thus, the so-called *"priority objectives"* announced in UNNADAF have been influenced by the OAU's submission. In addition, the OAU's goal and strategy of "collective self-reliance" were also clearly stated in UNNADAF.

3. Forecasts concerning the measures to be included in UNNADAF:

The divergence of views between the group of African countries and the group of capitalist developed countries (particularly the United States) was reflected by the different types of measures to be included in UNNADAF. As a result, some measures were drawn from the *African Alternative Framework to Structural Adjustment Programmes for Socio-Economic Recovery and Transformation (AAF-SAP)*, and some measures were related to the SAPs.

Thus, the most important measures drawn from the *AAF-SAP* were:

- "The implementation of policies for the transformation of the structure" of the African economies,[28] which means in fact implementation of the measures for import-substituting industrialization prescribed by the *AAF-SAP*, and

- "The promotion of regional and subregional economic cooperation and integration," including the "establishment of the African Economic Community," and the effective functioning of the existing cooperation and integration schemes, as prescribed by the *AAF-SAP*.[29]

And the most important measures related to the SAPs were:

- The continuation of "necessary reforms" and "improvement of domestic economic management, including effective mobilization and utilization of domestic resources,"[30] which means continuation of the SAPs sponsored by the Bretton Woods institutions.

In addition to these characteristic measures, UNNADAF contained also the following complementary measures:

- "Intensification of the democratization process," which means, according to the African submission, the "democratization of development" or "encouragement of the popular participation in development," and respect of "human and people's right,"[31]
- Promotion of investment through the creation of an "enabling environment" that would attract foreign and domestic direct investment,[32]
- The improvement of human rights and living standard, and human resource development,[33]
- Protection of the environment, including fight against desertification,[34]
- Implementation of population policies, under the Kilimandjaro Programme of Action for African Population and Self-Reliant Development, including reduction of maternal and child mortality, provisions for family planning and female education,[35]
- The promotion of agricultural and rural development, in order to achieve food safety,[36]
- Intensification of South-South cooperation,[37]
- Call for an increased role for non-governmental organizations (African and non-African),[38] and
- Call for increased international support, which includes solution of Africa's debt,[39] official development assistance

amounting to $30 billion in 1992 (which would need to grow at an average of 4 per cent per annum),[40] improvement of the market access to Africa's exports,[41] support for the diversification of the African economies,[42] reduction or removal of tariff and non-tariff barriers affecting African exports,[43] and support for the African regional economic integration.[44]

4. Forecasts concerning the expected behavior of the international community:

With regard to the expected behavior of the international community concerning its support for the implementation of UN-NADAF, the group of African countries appeared, once more, very optimistic. However, while most capitalist developed countries were silent about their respective positions concerning UNNADAF, the United States expressed some reservations regarding its understanding of the language of the new program.

The optimism of the group of African countries was clearly reflected by the address of the representative of Ghana to the 46th Ordinary Session of the UN General Assembly. Indeed, in response to the intervention of the representative of the United States, the representative of Ghana stated that:

[He] should like to thank the General Assembly for its support for [UNNADAF] and to express the wish that, when it comes to the implementation through the decade of the 1990s, of some of the prescriptions set forth in this [new program], we shall have our friends on board for Africa to make a move forward. (Provisional Verbatim Record of the 77th Meeting, 46th Session of the General Assembly, UN document No. A/46/PV.77 of 6 January 1992, pp. 23-24)

Contrary to this optimism of the group of African countries, the United States expressed a conditional support for the new program. Indeed, the US representative explicitly indicated that his country wanted Resolution 46/151 and its annex to recognize the link between "improved governance and accountability" and "successful and long-term development."[45] In other words, the United States wanted the African countries to focus on "good governance" and accountability, as the solution to their economic and social problems. In fact, that was not at all the main focus of UNNADAF, which concentrated on import-substituting industrialization (ISI), and promotion of regional cooperation and integration. Furthermore, the US representative also stated that his country would not "pressure private creditors to write off their [African] debts," nor would it bring into question the "financial integrity" of the Bretton Woods institutions, by suggesting the forgiveness of debts Africa owed to those institutions.[46] Besides, since good governance, accountability, and democracy became by the beginning of the 1990s the new conditions required by most capitalist developed countries for their assistance to developing countries, it was also predictable that the United States and its allies would not indiscriminately give assistance to all African countries. On the contrary, they would continue to support the African countries, which were applying SAPs and were democratizing.

The Adoption of UNNADAF

In addressing the question of how UNNADAF was adopted by the UN General Assembly, we need to analyze Resolution 46/151 and discuss the criteria that have been taken into consideration in the process of recommendation.

Established by resolution 45/178 of 19 December 1990,[47] the Ad Hoc Committee for the final review and appraisal of the implementation of UNPAAERD played an important role in drafting and recommending Resolution 46/151 and its annex to the UN General Assembly. This Ad Hoc Committee, chaired by Martin Huslid of Norway, conducted formal and informal meetings between September 3 and 14, 1991, and received the following documents:

- Africa's Submission on the Final Review and Appraisal on the Implementation of UNPAAERD,[48]
- Memorandum by the Conference of Ministers of the Economic Commission for Africa to the Ad Hoc Committee of the Whole of the General Assembly on the Final Review and Appraisal on the Implementation of UNPAAERD,[49]
- Report of the Secretary-General on the Critical Economic Situation in Africa: Final Review and Appraisal of the Implementation of UNPAAERD,[50] and
- Report of the Secretary-General on the Implementation of Diversification in the Commodity Sector in Africa.[51]

This list clearly shows that, contrary to UNPAAERD, the official contributions from non-African countries to the formulation and adoption of UNNADAF were rather limited, if not insignificant. In fact, the official records of the 46th Ordinary Session of the UN General Assembly revealed that only Norway made some amendments to Resolution 46/151 and its annex,[52] and only the United States addressed the UN General Assembly to explain its position on the adoption of this resolution.[53] Consequently, it can be argued that, more than UNPAAERD, UNNADAF was strongly influenced by the group of African countries.

Therefore, if we referred to the criteria for policy recommendation (i.e., effectiveness, efficiency, adequacy, equity, responsiveness, and appropriateness) suggested by policy analysts such as William Dunn (1994: 282-289), we can argue that the most important criteria that have been used in the recommendation of UNNADAF to the UN General Assembly was its *responsiveness* to the preferences of the group of African countries. Indeed, the potential effectiveness, efficiency, adequacy, equity and appropriateness of this new program were not at all taken into account during the meetings of the Ad Hoc Committee and the UN General Assembly.

The reason for this is that, by the end of the 1980s, the import-substituting industrialization (ISI), upon which UNNADAF was based, was failing in many developing countries, including Africa (Rapley, 1997; Spero and Hart, 1997). This should have led the African countries, the Ad Hoc Committee and the UN General Assembly to question the potential effectiveness, efficiency, adequacy, and appropriateness of this particular measure included in UNNADAF. Unfortunately, that was not the case.

Moreover, some serious questions should have been asked concerning the adoption of contradictory measures in UNNADAF. For instance, any policy maker or stake holder would have questioned the combination of the prescriptions of the ECA contained in the *AAF-SAP* (which called for unrestricted expenditures for investment and social services) with those of the World Bank and the IMF contained in the SAPs (which called for reduction of budget deficit and cuts in social services).

Furthermore, other questions should have been also asked concerning the belief held by many African political leaders and policy makers that the establishment of regional cooperation and integration (particularly the establishment of the African Economic Community) would spark economic growth and development in Africa. In fact, after more than 30 years of experience, none of the hundreds of African economic cooperation and integration schemes has been as successful as the European Economic Community (DeLancey and Mays, 1994; Fredland, 1990).

Finally, like UNPAAERD, UNNADAF was adopted *without vote* by the UN General Assembly. Understandably, this type of procedure for policy adoption was designed to speed up the adoption of some UN General Assembly resolutions. However, at the same time, it had some negative effects on the genuine commitment of member states, which were expected to comply with the provisions of a resolution adopted without their vote.   In fact, these negative effects surfaced with the implementation of UNNADAF, as most member states and international organizations did not comply with its prescriptions.

The Implementation and Evaluation of UNNADAF

In evaluating the implementation of UNNADAF, we need to look at the *policy actions* (i.e., inputs and processes) that took place under UNNADAF and their *consequences* (i.e., outputs and impacts). As with UNPAAERD, this analysis will allow us to see whether the African countries and the international community fully complied with the prescriptions of UNNADAF, which was also based on the concept of *global compact*.[54]

Concerning the policy inputs, in application of the concept of global compact, the African countries were committed under UNNADAF to improve their financial resource mobilization and allocation, while the international community was expected to provide increased ODA, to encourage the flows of FDI to Africa, and to find solutions to the African debt crisis.   Thus, in terms of inputs, the implementation UNNADAF heavily relied on the financial contribution of the international community.   Indeed, with regard to the ODA, Resolution 46/151, annex II.B, stipulated that:

> A critical element of the support from the international community is the provision of adequate resource flows to Africa [...]. To achieve an average annual growth rate of real gross national product of at least 6 per cent by African countries over the course of the 1990s the Secretary-General has estimated that a minimum of 30 billion dollars in net official development

Table 3.2 – Implementation of UNNADAF:
Available Financial Resources

Available Financial Resources	1986-1989	1990-1999
1 – Domestic Resources		
- Gross domestic savings (annual average as percentage of GDP)	21.2	17.3
- Gross domestic investment (annual average as percentage of GDP)	19.8	19.1
- Gross domestic investment (annual average in billions of dollars, in current prices)	76.4	93.4
2 – External Resources		
- Net official development assistance (annual average in billions of dollars, in current prices)	14.4	19.9
- Net official development assistance (annual average percentage growth rate, in current prices)	6.9	-17.2
- Net foreign direct investment (annual average in billions of dollars, in current prices)	2.1	4.1

Source: World Bank (2001).

Table 3.3 - Implementation of UNNADAF:
Economic and social conditions in Africa (1990-1999)

Economic and social Development Indicators	1985-1989	1990-1999
1 - Economic Growth		
- Annual average percentage growth rate of GDP (in constant 1995 prices)	2.5	2.4
- Annual average GNP per capita (in US dollars, Atlas method)	674	685
2 – Agricultural Development		
- Value added in agriculture (annual average percentage growth rate, in constant 1995 prices)	4.6	2.2
- Food import (annual average percentage growth rate, (in current prices)	10	0.3
3 - Industrial development		
- Value added in industry (annual average percentage growth rate, in constant 1995 prices)	1.8	1.8
4 - Social development		
- Adult literacy (percentage)	53	45.5
- Life expectancy at birth	50	54
5 - Economic stabilization		
- Budget deficit (as percentage of GDP)	-	-9.5
- Total external debt (annual average in billions of dollars, current prices)	228.4	302.6

Source: World Bank (2001).

assistance is required in 1992, after which the real net official development assistance would need to grow at an average rate of 4 percent per annum. (UN document No. A/RES/46/151 of 18 December 1991, annex II.B.2(b), parag.29)

In addition, the international community was also expected to "introduce measures and devise programmes to encourage direct foreign investment in African countries and support the policy changes undertaken by African countries to attract foreign investment."[55] Furthermore, it was expected to find "durable solutions to the African debt crisis."[56]

Contrary to their commitment to provide $82.5 billion or 64.4 per cent of the total cost of the implementation of UNPAAERD, the financial contributions of the African countries under UNNADAF were vaguely formulated as to "persist with necessary reforms and pursue improvement of domestic economic management, including effective mobilization and utilization of domestic resources."[57]

However, in comparing the financial resources available before and after the adoption of UNNADAF, we found that the expected financial resources were not available during the period of the implementation of UNNADAF (1990-1999).[58] Indeed, the net ODA to Africa did not reach the threshold of $30 billion a year by 1992, nor did it increase at the rate of 4 per cent a year thereafter. It is true that it increased, in current prices, from an average of $14.4 billion a year during the period of 1985-1989 to an average of $19.9 billion a year during the period of 1990-1999. However, this was far below the expected average of $30 billion a year. In fact, in current prices, it fell from a high of $24.3 billion in 1990 to as low as $14.1 billion in 1999 (World Bank, 2001: 284).[59]

With regard to the FDI, there was an increase, in constant 1987 prices, from an average of $2.1 billion a year during the period of 1985-1989 to $4.1 billion a year during the period of 1990-1999. However, despite this increase, the level of FDI to the Africa countries remained low, compared to that of the other developing countries in Asia and Latin America. Indeed, according to the UN Secretary-General, less than 2 per cent of the total FDI flows worldwide (or about 10 per cent of the total foreign direct investment flows to all developing countries) came to Africa since the beginning of the 1990s.[60] Furthermore, the UN Secretary-General noted that:

Foreign direct investment flows to Africa mainly concentrated on the petroleum industry which had the highest rates of return, notwithstanding the political instability, crisis and conflicts, in countries such as Angola. Nigeria and Egypt alone attracted nearly three quarters of foreign direct investment flows to petroleum-producing countries, accounting for 40 per cent of total foreign direct investment. (UN document No. A/51/228/ Add.1 of 29 July 1996, parag. 20.)

Concerning the African domestic financial resources, while the level of domestic savings, as a percentage of the gross domestic product (GDP), declined from 21.2 per cent during the period of 1986-1990 to 17.3 per cent during the period of 1990-1999, that of the domestic investment remained almost at the same level during both periods (19.8% in 1986-1990, and 19.1% in 1990-1999).[61]

With regard to the policy processes, in application of the concept of global compact, all "governments, organs, organizations and bodies of the UN system and intergovernmental and non-governmental organization [were requested] to take appropriate measures in order to implement the commitments contained in the New Agenda."[62] Thus, just as with UNPAAERD, there was no specific entity (individual or organization) designated to administer UNNADAF. Different structures have been used later to remedy this need for an administrator (or, at least, to play the role of program coordinator), such as the Office of the Special Coordinator for Africa and the Least Developed Countries,[63] and the Inter-agency Task Force for the Implementation of the UNNADAF.[64] However, none of these entities could fully play the role of program administrator, which could have taken control of the inputs and processes required for the implementation of UNNADAF.

Consequently, just as UNPAAERD before it, UNNADAF did not become the general framework for assistance by the international community to Africa, as the African countries expected. Instead, it had also to compete with the powerful SAPs sponsored by the Bretton Woods institutions and the capitalist developed countries.

Given the fact that the policy inputs and processes required for the implementation of UNNADAF did not come forth, and that the majority of African countries (at least, 29 of them) were actually applying the SAPs sponsored by the Bretton Woods institutions, it is not appropriate to consider the economic and social conditions of Africa during the period of 1990-1999 solely as the consequences of UNNADAF. Nevertheless, we need to refer to these economic and social conditions, in order to see whether the goals and objectives of UNNADAF were achieved, regardless of the fact that policy inputs and processes have been inadequate.[65]

The most specific objective of UNNADAF was to achieve an annual average growth rate of 6 per cent of the GDP at the level of the whole continent. On this account, as shown in Table 3.3, the objective of UNNADAF was totally missed, as the annual average growth rate of GDP remained at the same level during the period of 1985-1989 (2.5 per cent) and the period of 1990-1999 (2.4 per cent).[66] However, despite this stagnation, there was a relative increase of the annual average per capita GNP from $674 during the period of 1985-1989 to $685 during the period of 1990-1999.[67]

With regard to the objective of "accelerated transformation" (i.e., industrialization) of the African economies, the industrial sector was actually stagnating all over Africa, as the percentage growth rate of the value added in industry remained at the same level (1.8 per cent a year) as in the 1980s.[68] The situation was even worse in sub-Saharan Africa, where the share of the industrial sector as a percentage of the GDP dropped from 34 per cent in 1992 to 30 per cent in 1995, and the manufacturing sector dropped respectively from 17 per cent to 15 per cent (World Bank, 1997b, 1994a).

Nevertheless, there was some progress with regard to the integration of the African economies. Indeed, the Abuja Treaty establishing the African Economic Community came into force in 1993. In addition, other sub-regional organizations of cooperation and integration were created, especially the Common Market for Eastern and Southern Africa (COMESA), along with the Cross Border Initiative (CBI), which was also located in Eastern and Southern Africa.

The intensification of the integration of African economies was also demonstrated by the increase in the trade between African countries. Indeed, as a percentage of their total exports, the exports from sub-Saharan African countries to sub-Saharan African countries increased from an average of 1.9 per cent in 1987 to 7.4 per cent in 1997 (World Bank, 2001: 118-144).[69] However, these percentages were far below the percentage of exports between European Community countries (as the most economically integrated countries in the world), which averaged 62 per cent by 1997 (World Bank, 2001: 118-144). Therefore, Africa was still far from being economically integrated as it should have been by the end of 1990s.

The diversification of the African economies, which was also related to their transformation,[70] was one of the priority objectives of UNNADAF. Concerning the progress in this domain, the report of the Ad Hoc Committee for the mid-term review of the implementation of UNNADAF indicated that, despite the efforts made by African countries, most of them "still rely on a few primary commodities for much of their export earnings."[71] In addition, a proposal to establish a "Diversification Fund for Africa's Commodities" was abandoned by the UN General Assembly in 1995.[72] Thus, it can be argued that the objective of economic diversification was also missed.

Conclusion

Just as UNPAAERD before it, UNNADAF has been ineffective in dealing with the African economic and social problems in the 1990s. It failed to achieve most of its major objectives, particularly that of achieving 6 per cent annual growth rate of the GDP, and that of transforming and diversifying of the African economies. Some progress was made in terms of economic integration. However, Africa was still far away from being economically integrated by the end of the 1990s, as most African countries were still trading more with the rest of the world than among themselves.

In the same way as UNPAAERD, the formulation of UNNADAF was also strongly influenced by the group of African countries, which believed in an inward-looking development strategy based on the import-substituting industrialization (ISI) model and the concept of *collective self-reliance*. In order to accommodate the capitalist developed countries, UNNADAF also contained some measures drawn from the SAPs. However, it was the lack of policy actions (i.e., inputs and processes), characterized by the inadequacy of the financial resources and the non-compliance of almost all member states of the UN and all relevant international organizations, which completely hampered the implementation of UNNADAF and ultimately contributed to its total failure.

Notes

[1]   See Resolution 46/151 of 18 December 1991, UN document No. A/RES/46/151, the annex to which contains the United Nations New Agenda

for the Development of Africa in the 1990s (UNNADAF).
[2] See Africa's Submission on the Final Review and Appraisal of the Implementation of UNPAAERD, UN document No. A/46/387, annex, of 29 August 1991; the Memorandum by the Conference of Ministers of the Economic Commission for Africa on the Final Review and Appraisal of the Implementation of UNPAAERD, UN document No. A/46/280, annex, of 2 July 1991; the report UN Secretary-General on the final review and appraisal of UNPAAERD, UN document No. A/46/324 of 6 August 1991; and the UN General Assembly resolution on the final review and appraisal of UNPAAERD, UN document No. A/46/324 of 6 August 1991, annex I.
[3] UN document No. A/46/324 of 6 August 1991, foreword by the Secretary-General, p. 3.
[4] According to the World Bank, the per capita GNP for all Africa declined from $673 in 1985 to $664 in 1990, that is a rate of decline of about 0.2 per cent a year (World Bank, 1995: 34).
[5] According to the World Bank, the annual average percentage growth rate of food imports rose from 0.1 per year in 1980-1985 to 3.3 per cent a year in 1986-1992 (World Bank, 1995: 109). A report of the UN Secretary General indicates also that "Food aid needs of the 45 countries of sub-Saharan Africa increased by more than 45 per cent in 1987-1988, from the level of previous year, and 1989 cereal import requirements rose further by 3.8 per cent" (UN document No. A/46/324 of 6 August 1991, p. 62, parag. 228).
[6] According to the World Bank, the total external debt of all Africa increased, in current prices, from $209 billion in 1986 to $278 billion in 1991 (World Bank, 1995: 172).
[7] The report of the Secretary-General indicates that desertification, deforestation and soil degradation continued during the period of 1986-1990 (UN document No. 46/324 of 6 August 1991, p. 26, parag. 95).
[8] UN document No. A/RES/46/151 of 18 December 1991, annex I.A, parag. 10.
[9] UN document No. A/RES/46/151 of 18 December 1991, annex I.A, parag. 11.
[10] *Ibid..*
[11] *Ibid..*
[12] *Ibid..*
[13] See Table 3.1 - The Different Interpretations of the Causes of the Critical Economic and Social Conditions in Africa in the 1990s, below, p. 44.
[14] UN document No. A/46/387 of 29 August 1991.
[15] See Table 3.1 - The Different Interpretations of the Causes of the Critical Economic and Social Conditions in Africa in the 1990s, below, p. 44.
[16] The *African Alternative Framework to Structural Adjustment Programmes for Socio-Economic Recovery and Transformation (AAF-SAP)* was adopted by the Conference of Ministers of the Economic Commission for Africa in April

1989, and later officially endorsed by the Assembly of Heads of State and Government of the OAU. See UN document No. A/44/315 of 21 June 1989, annex; or E/ECA/CM.15/6/Rev.3.

[17] As mentioned earlier, structuralist theory was initially developed by such analysts as Raul Prebish (1950), and Hans Singer (1950); and dependency theory was a "second generation of structuralism," developed by such analysts as Andre Gunder Frank (1967), Samir Amin (1967), and Fernando Cardoso and Enzo Faletto (1979).   The major difference between the two theories of development is that the former favored official development assistance and foreign direct investment to developing countries as means of development, while the latter prescribed "autonomous national-development strategies," which would require the developing countries to "sever their ties to the world economy and [to] become more self-sufficient" (Rapley, 1996: 18-20).

[18] Address by Mr. Marks (United States of America), UN document No. A/46/PV.77, pp. 21-23.

[19] See UN documents No. A/46/L.53 of 16 December 1991, and No. A/46/L.56 of 17 December 1991, amendments by Norway.

[20] In its first amendment (UN documents No. A/46/L.53), Norway proposed some modifications in the formulation of Resolution 46/151, annex II.B.2, paragraphs 25, 26 and 27.   These modifications tend toward a call for additional debt relief and additional development assistance in favor of the African countries. In its second amendment (UN documents No. A/46/L.56), Norway suggested adding to Resolution 46/151 paragraphs 3 and 4, which concerned the responsibility of member states, international organizattions and the UN Secretary- General.

[21] See Table 3.1 - The Different Interpretations of the Causes of the Critical Economic and Social Conditions in Africa in the 1990s, above, p. 42.

[22] *Ibid..*

[23] As noted in chapter 2, section 2.2, by the end of the 1980s, the number of adjusting countries was 29, and that of non-adjusting countries 19.

[24] *Ibid.*, parag. 5. (Given the fact that the difference between GNP and GDP is not significant for most developing countries, and that most useful sources refer actually to the growth of GDP, we will refer to the annual growth of the GDP, instead of the annual growth of GNP, as suggested by this UN document).

[25] UN document No. A/RES/46/151, annex II.A, parag. 1.

[26] UN document No. A/RES/46/151, annex II.A, parag. 7.

[27] UN document No. A/46/387 of 29 August 1991, annex, parag. 12.

[28] UN document No. A/RES/46/151 of 18 December 1991, annex II.B.1(a), parag.10.

[29] UN document No. A/RES/46/151 of 18 December 1991, annex II.B.1(b), parag.11.

[30] *Ibid..*

[31] UN document No. A/RES/46/151 of 18 December 1991, annex II.B.1(c),

parag.13.
[32] UN document No. A/RES/46/151 of 18 December 1991, annex II.B.1(d), parag.14. (This is a very important element of the SAPs).
[33] UN document No. A/RES/46/151 of 18 December 1991, annex II.B.1(e), parag.15 and 16.
[34] UN document No. A/RES/46/151 of 18 December 1991, annex II.B.1(f), parag. 17.
[35] UN document No. A/RES/46/151 of 18 December 1991, annex II.B.1(g), parag.18.
[36] UN document No. A/RES/46/151 of 18 December 1991, annex II.B.1(h), parag. 19.
[37] UN document No. A/RES/46/151 of 18 December 1991, annex II.B.1(i), parag. 20.
[38] UN document No. A/RES/46/151 of 18 December 1991, annex II.B.1(j), parag. 21.
[39] UN document No. A/RES/46/151 of 18 December 1991, annex II.B.2(a), parag. 23-28.
[40] UN document No. A/RES/46/151 of 18 December 1991, annex II.B.2(b), parag. 29-30.
[41] UN document No. A/RES/46/151 of 18 December 1991, annex II.B.2(c), parag. 31-32.
[42] UN document No. A/RES/46/151 of 18 December 1991, annex II.B.2(d), parag. 33-35.
[43] UN document No. A/RES/46/151 of 18 December 1991, annex II.B.2(e), parag. 36.
[44] UN document No. A/RES/46/151 of 18 December 1991, annex II.B.2(f), parag. 37-38.
[45] Address by Mr. Marks (United States of America), Provisional Verbatim Record of the 77th Meeting, 46th Session of the General Assembly, UN document No. A/46/PV.77 of 6 January 1992, pp. 21-23.
[46] *Ibid.*.
[47] UN document A/RES/45/178 of 19 December 1990.
[48] UN document No. A/46/387 of 29 August 1991, annex.
[49] UN document No. A/46/280 of 2 July 1991, annex.
[50] UN document No. A/46/324 of 6 August 1991.
[51] UN document No. A/46/324/Add.1 of 14 August 1991.
[52] UN documents No. A/46/L.53 of 16 December 1991, and A/46/L.56 of 17 December 1991. As mentioned earlier, these amendments did not substantially change the contents and the language of Resolution 46/151 and its annex.
[53] Address by Mr. Marks (United States of America), Provisional Verbatim Record of the 77th Meeting, 46th Session of the General Assembly, UN document No. A/46/PV.77 of 6 January 1992, pp. 21-23.

[54]   See the definition and implications of the concept of global compact in Chapter 1, pp. 1-2.

[55]   UN document No. A/RES/46/151 of 18 December 1991, annex II.B.2(b), parag. 30.

[56]   UN document No. A/RES/46/151 of 18 December 1991, annex II.B.2(a), parag. 23-28.

[57]   UN document No. A/RES/46/151 of 18 December 1991, annex II.B.1(a), parag.10.

[58]   See Table 3.2 – Implementation of UNNADAF: Available Financial Resources, above, p. 55.

[59]   *Ibid..*

[60]   Report of the Secretary-General on the Implementation of UNNADAF, UN document No. A/51/228/Add.1 of 29 July 1996, parag. 20.

[61]   See Table 3.2 – Implementation of UNNADAF: Available Financial Resources, above, p. 55.

[62]   UN document No. 46/151 of 18 December 1991, parag. 3.

[63]   The Secretary-General was invited in 1993 to reinforce the capability of this Office in order to "follow up, monitor and evaluate [the] implementation of the New Agenda."   See UN document No. A/RES/48/214 of 11 January 1994, parag. 10.

[64]   This Task Force was for instance invited in 1994 to "make available advisory services to the African Development Bank on the questions related to the diversification of Africa's commodities." See UN document A/RES/49/142 of 3 February 1995, parag. 16.

[65]   See Table 3.3 - Implementation of UNNADAF: Economic and social conditions in Africa (1990-1999), above, p. 56.

[66]   *Ibid..*

[67]   *Ibid..*

[68]   *Ibid..*

[69]   We do not have the data concerning North Africa and the whole African continent here.

[70]   Economic transformation (or industrialization) is presented by some UN documents as a "vertical diversification." See UN document No. A/51/48 of 27 September 1996, parag. 78(b).

[71]   UN document No. A/51/48 of 27 September 1996, parag. 77.

[72]   The establishment of this fund was recommended by the Secretary-General in 1993 (UN document A/48/335 of 2 October 1993). However, instead of creating this fund, the UN General Assembly, through resolution 49/142 of 3 February 1995, invited the existing financial institutions (particularly, the African Development Bank, the World bank and the IMF) and the developed countries to pay attention and to accord high priority to the diversification of African commodities (UN document No. A/RES/49/142 of 3 February 1995, parag. 12-14).

Chapter 4

The Internal Causes of the Failure
of UNPAAERD and UNNADAF

After having analyzed the formulation, adoption, implementation and evaluation of the two UN development programs (UNPAAERD and UNNADAF), in Chapters 2 and 3, this chapter identifies and analyzes the internal causes of the failure of these programs. These internal causes, also described as "limitations" or "institutional weakness" of the United Nations by some analysts (Puchala, 1996; Gwin and Williams, 1996), relate to the functioning of the UN as an agency of international development, formulating and implementing its own development programs.

Since the formulation and recommendation of UNPAAERD and UNNADAF were strongly influenced by the group of African countries within the UN General Assembly, one may wonder if the failure of these two UN development programs can be simply explained by the way the group of African countries formulated them. However, this explanation would not take into consideration the way the UN General Assembly itself adopted and implemented these programs. Therefore, in order to explain fully the internal causes of failure of the two UN development programs, we need to identify any flaw, not only in the processes of their formulation and recommendation, but also in the processes of their adoption, implementation and evaluation within the UN General Assembly.

Identification of Wrong Policy Problems

In order to understand the failure of the two UN development programs with respect to the identification of the policy problems, we need to focus on how the group of African countries interpreted the causes of the African critical economic and social conditions in the 1980s and 1990s. The analyses of the proposals submitted by the group of African countries, in Chapters 2 and 3, demonstrated that this group consistently argued that the main economic problem of Africa was the "lack of structural transformation" (i.e., lack of industrialization), which led to the dependence of the African economies on the world economy, and to their vulnerability to external shocks (particularly, the economic recessions in the developed countries, and the deterioration of the terms of trade).[1]

This type of argument has not changed since the adoption of the *Monrovia Strategy for the Economic Development of Africa* by the OAU in July 1979. The *Monrovia Strategy* was further developed into the famous *Lagos Plan of Action for the Implementation of the Monrovia Strategy for the Economic Development of Africa*, also known as the *Lagos Plan of Action (LPA)*,[2] which was adopted by the OAU in April 1980. All subsequent African development strategies and programs (either developed by the OAU itself or the ECA) were based on the *LPA*, particularly the two programs that have been used in the formulation of UNPAAERD and UNNADAF, respectively: (1) *Africa's Priority Programme for Economic Recovery 1986-1990 (APPER)*, adopted by the OAU in July 1985; and (2) the *African Alternative Framework to Structural Adjustment Programmes for Socio-Economic Recovery and Transformation (AAF-SAP)*,[3] adopted by the Conference of Ministers of the Economic Commission for Africa in April 1989, and later endorsed by the OAU.

All of these African development strategies and programs were based on the concept of *collective self-reliance*, which was justified in the preamble of the *LPA* as follows:

> The effect of unfulfilled promises of global development strategies has been more sharply felt in Africa than in the other Continents of the world. Indeed rather than result in an improvement in the economic situation of the continent, successive strategies have made the continent stagnate and become more susceptible than other regions to the economic and social crises suffered by the industrialised countries. Thus, Africa is unable to point to any significant growth rate or satisfactory index of general well-being in the last twenty years. Faced with this situation and determined to undertake measures for the basic restructuring of the economic base of our continent, we resolved to adopt a far-reaching regional approach based primarily on *collective self-reliance*. (UN document No. A/S-11/14 of 21 August 1980, annex I, preamble, parag. 1) (Emphasis added)

Many analysts, particularly John Ravenhill (1986b), think that the *LPA*'s goal and strategy of *collective self-reliance* were unrealistic. In this sense, John Ravenhill even disparages the concept of *collective self-reliance* contained in the *LPA* as a "collective self-delusion." As he puts it:

> the [Lagos] plan appears to be little more than a plea for externally-financed self-reliance. Rather than meeting the costs of development from internally generated resources, international donors are expected to foot the bill. (Ravenhill, 1986b: 89)

Other analysts, like Timothy Shaw (1986), try to understand the *LPA*'s goal and strategy of *collective self-reliance* in the context of the theoretical debate on development, and argue that these goal and strategy were in fact based on the application of the dependency theory to the African development problems, which led to the prescriptions of import-substituting industrialization (ISI), regional cooperation and integration, and delinkage of the African economies from the world economy (i.e., self-reliance).

In analyzing the *LPA* in the light of the major development theories (Rapley, 1996; Spero and Hart, 1997), we found that it was in reality a product of a combination of structuralist theory and dependency theory of development. Indeed, the *LPA* contains the argument commonly shared by both structuralists and dependency theorists. According to this argument, in the context of the international division of labor between capitalist developed countries (producers of manufactured goods) and developing countries (producers of raw materials), "the international market structure perpetuates the backwardness and dependency" of the developing countries, while it "encourages the dominance" by the capitalist developed countries (Spero and Hart, 1997: 154-155). In connection with this argument, the *LPA* contains the prescriptions of both the structuralists and the dependency theorists. Taking into consideration the structuralist prescriptions, it suggests such measures as import-substituting industrialization (ISI), regional cooperation and integration, along with the acceptance of external resource flows (particularly ODA and FDI); and, following dependency theory prescriptions, it advocates at the same time the delinkage of the African economies from the world economy, and the adoption of the goal and strategy of collective self-reliance.

There were, however, two major problems with this application of structuralist theory and/or dependency theory in analyzing the African economic and social problems in the 1980s and 1900s. First, this approach led to a sweeping generalization of a situation that was not applicable to all African countries.   Second, while economic dependence and vulnerability may have constituted the major obstacles to the development of some African countries, these factors were not in fact the main causes of the critical economic and social conditions in Africa in the 1980s and 1990s.

Different studies (particularly, Barro, 1997; Easterly and Levine, 1997; Rapley, 1996; World Bank, 1994, 1984, 1981) revealed in fact that the major causes of the economic and social conditions in Africa during this period were:

- Political instability and/or armed conflicts,
- Economic mismanagement and/or adoption of inadequate economic policies, and
- Droughts or deterioration of the environment.

The adoption of both structuralist theory and dependency theory led the African political leaders and policy makers to overlook these important factors.

Taking into consideration these factors, we can classify the African countries in the 1980s and 1990s into four different groups:

1. A group of countries devastated by political instability and/or protracted armed conflicts,
2. A group of countries ruined by economic mismanagement and/or inadequate economic policies, or simply governed by autocratic or "predatory kleptocrat" political leaders (Raven-hill, 1986a),
3. A group of countries devastated by droughts or severe deterioration of the environment, and
4. A group of remaining African countries which were not affected by any of the above factors.

1.   The group of African countries devastated severe political instability and/or protracted armed conflicts: Most of these countries were simply described by analysts as "failed states" or "stateless countries," because of the collapse of the state and the non-existence of functioning governments in those countries (Lyons, 1995; Mazrui, 1995). According to Wallensteen and Axell (1994: 335), there was an annual average of 14 armed conflicts within or between African countries by the end of the 1980s and at the beginning of the 1990s, with a peak of 17 in 1990 and 1991. During the 1980s and 1990s, this group included such countries as: Algeria, Angola, Burundi, Chad, Ethiopia, Liberia, Mozambique, Niger, Rwanda, Sierra Leone, Somalia, Sudan, and Uganda. Since armed conflict and/or political instability negatively affect the economic growth and development of any given country in the world (Easterly and Levine, 1997; Fosu, 1992), it can be argued that the critical economic and social conditions in many African countries in the 1980s and 1990s were caused, not so much by their economic dependence and vulnerability, as by the severe political instability and/or armed conflicts, which prevented consistent economic activities in those countries. It can be argued also that the poor economic performance of these war-torn and unstable countries affected the aggregate data concerning the continent as a whole. Therefore, the application of structuralist theory and/or dependency theory to explain the critical economic and social conditions in Africa was inappropriate and misleading, because it did not consider political instability and/or armed conflicts as major causes of poor economic performance.

2. *The group of African countries ruined by economic mis-management and/or inadequate economic policies, or governed by autocratic or "predatory kleptocrat" political leaders*: The leaders of these countries generally cared little about the welfare of their people. As Hess and Ross (1994) pointed out, there are no "truly functioning governments," that is, governments that could deliver public services in countries run by autocratic or predatory political leaders. Many African countries could be included in this group, but the typical cases during the 1980s and 1990s were: Nigeria (under its different military rulers) and Zaire (under Mobutu Sese Seko). Since lack of "good governance" negatively affects the economic growth and development of any given country in the world (Barro, 1997; Easterly and Levine, 1997; World Bank, 1992), it can be argued that the major cause of the poor economic performance in these countries was economic mismanagement or lack of good governance, rather than their economic dependence and vulnerability. Once again, the application of structuralist theory and/or dependency theory to explain the critical economic and social conditions in these countries was inappropriate

and misleading, because it did not consider the lack of good governance as a major a cause of poor economic performance in many African countries.

   3. The group of African countries devastated by droughts or severe deterioration of the environment: This group included not only the Sahelian countries (Burkina Faso, Chad, Mali, Mauritania, and Niger), but also some Eastern and Southern African countries (Ethiopia, Somalia, Zambia, and Zimbabwe).   The mass poverty, hunger and famine in most of these countries were generally explained by the existence of permanent droughts or severe deterioration of the environment, not by their economic dependence and vulnerability (Mortimore, 1989).   Therefore, the application of structuralist theory and/or dependency theory was once again inappropriate and misleading, because it did not consider permanent droughts or severe deterioration of the environment as major causes of poor economic performance in these African countries.

   4. The group of remaining African countries: These countries did not suffer from political instability and/or armed conflicts, droughts or deterioration of the environment, and where normal or functioning governments existed and cared, more or less, about the welfare of the people. During the 1980s and 1990s, the group included such countries as Benin, Botswana, Cameroon, Côte d' Ivoire, Egypt, Gabon, Ghana, Kenya, Madagascar, Mauritius, Senegal, Tanzania, Tunisia.   While some of these countries achieved notable economic and social development after their independence (particularly, Botswana, Cameroon, Gabon, Mauritius and Tunisia), most of them have stagnated, if they did not declined since the 1970s (particularly Madagascar and Tanzania).

   It was in this last group of countries that the problems of a lack of structural transformation, along with economic dependence and vulnerability could have explained the critical economic and social conditions in the 1980s and 1990s.   However, even in most of these countries, dependence on the world economy and vulnerability to external shocks were not the major factors accounting for the critical economic and social conditions in the 1980s and 1990s. As a matter of fact, Africa as a whole was increasingly marginalized from the world economy since the 1970s (Callaghy, 1995; World Bank, 1994b, 1989a). It has been less exploited by multinational corporations (MNCs), and has produced far less for the world market, compared to other developing regions in the world.   Therefore, if the structuralists and dependency theorists were correct, Africa should have become less dependent on the world market and less vulnerable to external shocks, and should have significantly developed since the 1970s.

Unfortunately, that was not the case. In fact, instead of suffering from its dependence on the world economy and its vulnerability to external shocks, Africa was actually suffering from the stagnation and decline of its economy, which led to its marginalization from the world economy. As Thomas Callaghy correctly puts it:

> Africa generates a declining share of world output. The main commodities it produces are becoming less and less important or are being more efficiently produced by other Third World countries. Trade is declining, nobody wants to lend, and few want to invest except in narrowly defined mineral enclave sectors. (Callaghy, 1995: 42)

In addition, the World Bank also found that because of the low returns from investment on the continent, Africa was becoming less attractive not only for foreign investors, but also for domestic investors (World Bank, 1981). This led to the phenomenon of disinvestment in many African countries since the 1970s, as many African investors were increasingly moving their investments out of the continent.

Thus, contrary to the argument of the structuralists and/or dependency theorists followed by the African political leaders and policy makers, the critical economic and social conditions in Africa in the 1980s and 1990s were caused less by the economic dependence and vulnerability of Africa to external shocks than by armed conflicts and/or political instability, economic mismanagement and/or inadequate economic policies, and permanent droughts or deterioration of the environment. The inappropriate application of structuralist theory and/or dependency theory to explain these critical economic and social conditions led the African political leaders and policy makers to identify the wrong policy problems of "lack of structural transformation" (i.e., lack of industrialization), economic dependence and vulnerability, as the main causes of these conditions.

Formulations of Wrong Solutions

As the formulation of UNPAAERD and UNNADAF was strongly influenced by the group of African countries within the UN General Assembly, we need to focus on the solutions suggested by this group, in order to understand the failure of these two UN development programs with respect to their formulation. In fact, the formulation of these programs was handicapped not only by the identification of wrong policy problems (as demonstrated in the previous section), but also by the inaccurate forecasts made by the group of African countries concerning:

1. The consequences of the existing development programs in Africa (i.e., the SAPs),
2. The expected consequences (i.e., goals and objectives) of the two UN development programs (UNPAAERD and UN-NADAF),
3. The measures to be included in these two UN development programs in order to solve the African problems, and
4. The expected behavior of the relevant stakeholders, particularly the capitalist developed countries and the Bretton Woods institutions.

Having identified the "lack of structural transformation" (i.e., lack of industrialization), economic vulnerability and dependence as the main causes of the critical economic and social conditions in Africa in the 1980s and 1990s, the group of African countries consistently argued that the SAPs sponsored by the Bretton Woods institutions and the capitalist developed countries were not appropriate for addressing the African economic and social problems. The group of African countries forecasted that pursuing the SAPs would further aggravate the critical economic and social conditions in Africa. Thus, summarizing the negative consequences of the SAPs, particularly in the social domain, the *African Alternative Framework to Structural Adjustment Programmes* (*AAF-SAP*), formulated by the Economic Commission for Africa (ECA), stated that:

> The major transitional adverse social consequences of structural adjustment programme are: declining per capita income and real wages; rising unemployment and underemployment; deterioration in the level of social services as a result of cuts on social public expenditures; falling educational and training standards; rising malnutrition and health problems; and rising poverty levels and income inequalities. (UN document No. A/44/315 of 21 June 1989, annex, p. 24, parag. 68)

In line with this statement, the ECA drew the conclusion that the SAPs were "theoretically and empirically" flawed, and that there was an "*urgent need for an alternative*," which would "have to take into consideration, among other things, the structure of production and consumption and the people who are the main actors in the development process."[4]

However, notwithstanding the social and political costs of the SAPs, the forecasts made by the group of African countries about the totally negative consequences of these programs were inaccurate. Even by the end of the 1980s, when it was fashionable to talk about "adjustment with human face,"[5] the ECA's conclusion and the need to replace the SAPs altogether were not supported by strong evidence. As a matter of fact, even the UNDP had to agree with its "rival organization," the World Bank,[6] in a rare joint report in 1989 that:

> when the performance of reforming [or adjusting] countries is compared with that of non-reforming [or non-adjusting] countries, there is evidence that the combination of reforms and added assistance has led to higher agricultural growth, faster export, stronger GDP growth, and larger investment – this, despite the less favorable terms of trade facing the reforming countries. (World Bank and UNDP, 1989: 3)

Thus, contrary to the forecasts of the ECA and the OAU, several World Bank reports (particularly, World Bank, 1994b) and even the UN General Assembly Resolution 46/151,[7] as well as many other studies (among others, Shan, Ed. 1994), confirmed the positive impacts of the SAPs for "adjusting African countries" (but not for Africa as a whole). Therefore, if the SAPs were working and had some positive impacts on the economic and social conditions of the adjusting African countries, the "urgent need" to replace these programs claimed by the ECA and the OAU was not justified.

So why did the group of African countries insist on the replacement of the SAPs with UNPAAERD and UNNADAF? In addition to the alleged high social and political costs of the SAPs, mentioned earlier, one of the most important reasons which motivated many African political leaders and policy makers to find an alternative to the SAPs and to push their agenda through the UN General Assembly had to do with the notion of "political independence" and "national sovereignty." This concern was clearly expressed by the Secretary-General of the OAU in his 1982 report on the World Bank. Commenting on the *Accelerated Development in Sub-Saharan Africa* published by the World Bank in 1981, the OAU Secretary-General stated that:

the proposed outward-looking, external-oriented concept of development
proposed for our countries in the [World Bank 1981] report is indeed a
suggestion that we continue to do what we have been doing all these years.
The only difference is that *we lose the independence to set our goals,
adopt our strategy and determine our policies.* Added to this is the glaring
arrogant paternalism in the report with no concern shown for the need to
increase the capacity of our countries to do in the near future what
outsiders are doing for them now. (*Report of the Secretary-General of the
OAU on the World Bank Report,* quoted in Shaw, 1986: 108) (Emphasis
added)

In connection with this, Albert Zafy, a former President of
Madagascar, simply viewed the SAP implemented in his country as an
"affront to the national sovereignty" (Brown, 1997). As we will see in
the case of this country, in Chapter 6, this view was shared by a large
group of political leaders and policy makers, and constituted a major
obstacle for the pursuit of the implementation of the SAP, which has
been somewhat beneficial for the country.[8]

In other words, it was more the concern about losing their political
independence and national sovereignty than the actual consequences of
the SAPs that motivated many African political leaders and policy
makers to look for the replacement of these programs with the two UN
development programs.

The analyses of the *Lagos Plan of Action* and other African
development programs (especially *APPER* and *AAF-SAP*), which have
strongly influenced the formulation of UNPAAERD and UNNADAF,
revealed also that African political leaders and policy makers have
consistently argued that the ultimate goal of their development efforts
was the achievement the *"national and regional collective self-
reliance."* Thus, in order to understand the failure of the two UN
development programs, with respect to their goals and objectives, we
need also to analyze this concept of *collective self-reliance.*

As mentioned earlier, the adoption of the goal of *collective self-
reliance* – which was at the same time used as a development strategy –
was due to the application of structuralist theory and/or dependency
theory in interpreting the causes of the critical economic and social
conditions in Africa in the 1980s and 1990s. The application of these
theories led the African political leaders and policy makers to assume
that the economic and social problems of Africa were the result of the
domination and exploitation of the continent by the capitalist developed

countries, which made the African economies both dependent on the economies of these countries and vulnerable to external shocks. Therefore, the African political leaders and policy makers believed that in order to develop Africa, they would have to address these problems of capitalist domination and exploitation, economic dependence and vulnerability to external shocks, through *collective self-reliance*.

However, as John Ravenhill (1986) pointed out, the African political leaders and policy makers were not able to define in any detail *self-reliance* itself, "beyond the 'basic guidelines' outlined in the preamble to the [Lagos] plan" (Ravenhill, 1986b: 89). Furthermore, the author noted that "self-reliance," as it was used in the *LPA*, did not imply "internally-generated resources" for development, but instead "a plea for externally-financed self-reliance" (Ravenhill, 1986b: 89). This was because Africa simply had no means to pursue the goal and strategy of *collective self-reliance*. Therefore, the implementation of the *LPA* itself was based on the expectation that the international community would "foot the bill." In other words, there was a blatant contradiction between the goal and strategy of *collective self-reliance* and the means to achieve it. *Collective self-reliance*, both as a goal and a strategy, was simply unrealistic.

In addition to the identification of wrong problems, the integration of these unrealistic goal and strategy of *collective self-reliance* into the two UN development programs made them irremediably ineffective. Instead of directly addressing the crucial problems of Africa, such as armed conflicts, political instability, droughts, deterioration of the environment, lack of good governance, and economic mismanagement, these two UN development programs were formulated to solve the problems of capitalist domination and exploitation, along with the economic dependence and vulnerability of the continent. The development of the agriculture and the sectors in support of the agriculture under UNPAAERD, and the pursuit of import-substituting industrialization and regional cooperation and integration under UNNADAF, were geared toward solving these wrong problems.

To make the matter worse, even the most important measures adopted under the two UN development programs were not appropriate to promote sustainable economic and social development anywhere in the world in the 1980s and 1990s. First, the development of the agriculture and the sectors in support of the agriculture under UNPAAERD can be achieved successfully, and can lead in fact to food self-sufficiency and self-reliance. However, as demonstrated by the case of India in the 1960s, this development strategy can be very expensive, and may generate some unintended consequences (Rapley, 1996). In line with this, while recognizing the success of the so-called "Green Revolution" in India, John Rapley reported that:

> The Green Revolution also drew criticism. Because the new technologies were expensive and required high and regular water inputs, they were frequently accessible only to richer farmers, and thereby worsened rural inequalities. Moreover, as crop yields expanded, prices dropped, and many farmers were driven off the land. (Rapley, 1996: 34)

In other words, developing the agriculture and the sectors in support of the agriculture in order to achieve food self-sufficiency and self-reliance may not be a good development strategy for Africa, because of these economic and social costs. In fact, in some African countries, especially those in the desert area, agriculture could not be developed at all, no matter what the costs would have been. Therefore, instead of investing heavily in the agricultural sector, as prescribed in UNPAAERD, many African countries would have been better off in investing in other sectors of their economy (industry, manufacture or services), in which they could have had some comparative advantage.

Second, by the 1980s, it was widely acknowledged that the import-substituting industrialization (ISI) model (i.e., the type of Indus-trialization based on inward-looking strategy and aiming at the satisfaction of national or regional demands) was not an effective development strategy. In fact, this type of industrialization prescribed by UNNADAF was already failing in many African countries, as well as in many other developing countries in Asia and Latin America (Spero and Hart, 1997; Rapley, 1996; Cox, 1987). In explaining the failure of this development strategy, John Rapley correctly notes that:

> The [ISI] approach had been directed, intentionally, at physical-capital formation, and *neglected to foster competitiveness, innovation, technological capability, and other features of development*. With its focus on savings and investment, ISI proved very effective at building factories and infrastructure. In other regards, though, it was failing. (Rapley, 1996: 39) (Emphasis added)

Thus, according to the author, the main reason why the ISI model failed was that it did not foster the "competitiveness, innovation, technological capability, and other features of development" that could have made it as successful as the other model, known as the export-led growth (ELG) model. As we will see in the cases of Madagascar and Mauritius, the ISI model can also be very expensive and can tremendously increase the external debt of the country. Most countries, which have adopted this strategy, inefficiently produced goods that could not be exported to other countries because of their low quality of production. At the same time, they still had to import other goods, and did not always have the hard currency to pay for them. This situation generated both chronic deficits in the balance of payments and huge external debts for those countries. This is why many developing countries in East Asia and Latin America that have adopted an outward-looking development strategy based on the so-called export-led growth (ELG) model have been more successful than those having pursued the inward-looking development strategy based on the ISI model (Spero and Hart, 1997; Rapley, 1996; and Cox, 1987).

Finally, with regard to the complementary measures included in UNPAAERD and UNNADAF, particularly those related to the SAPs, some of these measures could have in fact improved the economic and social conditions of some African countries. However, they were not the main focus of the two UN development programs, and might have been adopted by the group of African countries in order to get the support of the capitalist developed countries and the Bretton Woods institutions. The *AAF-SAP* itself, which strongly influenced UN-NADAF, was designed as an alternative to the SAPs. This clearly indicates that the group of African countries had no intention at all to implement the complementary measures related to the SAPs.

The group of African countries made another major mistake when it forecasted that the whole international community would fully comply with the provisions of the two UN development programs. As the analysis of the implementation of each one of these programs demonstrated, neither the capitalist developed countries nor the Bretton Woods institutions, which controlled the bulk of ODA, complied with the provisions of these programs. As a result, they did not become the general frameworks for assistance to Africa, as the group of African countries had expected.

The African political leaders and policy makers believed that it would be easy to get the compliance of the capitalist developed countries and the Bretton Woods institutions by having the UN General Assembly adopt the two UN development programs. A similar belief was also reflected in the demand for a *New International Economic*

Order (NIEO) by the developing countries in the 1970s (Waelde, 1995; Cox, 1979). In the cases of UNPAAERD and UNNADAF, the African political leaders and policy makers wanted to bypass the constraints imposed by the Bretton Woods institutions by substituting these institutions with the UN and, at the same time, replacing the SAPs with these two UN development programs, which they expected to become the general frameworks for international assistance to Africa.

However, the capitalist developed countries and the Bretton Woods institutions had no interest in implementing these two UN development programs formulated against their own development programs for Africa (i.e., the SAPs), as well as against the prevailing world economic order, which they wanted to preserve. As a result, the two UN development programs did not become the general frameworks for international assistance to Africa, as expected by the group of African countries.

Flawed Processes of Policy Recommendation and Adoption

A broader explanation of the failure of UNPAAERD and UNNADAF has to take into consideration the processes of policy recommendation and adoption within the UN General Assembly. These processes were flawed and did not contribute to the adoption of the most potentially effective development programs. There were two major factors that led to this situation:

1. The only criterion of policy recommendation and adoption used for the adoption of the two UN development programs was the criterion of *responsiveness*; and
2. The procedure of *adoption without vote*, which was used in the cases of these programs, allowed their adoption even though some member states suspected their potential ineffectiveness and were opposed to their adoption.

First, since the adoption of resolution 40/40 on December 2, 1985, which convened the 13th Special Session of the UN General Assembly in 1986 and led to the adoption of UNPAAERD, the only criterion used for choosing a development program for Africa was the need to take "fully into account" the priorities set by the OAU.[9] Most African representatives at the UN consistently referred to this provision in their interventions to the UN General Assembly and during the sessions of the different committees devoted to the two UN development programs. Consequently, any development program that did not respond to this unique criterion, no matter how effective it could be, was automatically dismissed.

Obviously, the negative effect of this practice was that many alternative development programs have been rejected without any discussion concerning their potential effectiveness, efficiency, and appropriateness. Only the two African development programs (*APPER* and *AAF-SAP*), which perfectly took "fully into account" the priorities set by the OAU (even though they were potentially ineffective), were recommended to the UN General Assembly for adoption. In other words, the two UN development programs failed because the group of African countries failed to design the most effective development programs, and the processes of policy recommendation and adoption within the UN General Assembly did not prevent the adoption such potentially ineffective development programs.

Second, the UN Charter provides that decisions on economic and social questions such as those concerning UNPAAERD and UNNADAF can be "made by a majority of the members present and voting."[10] However, as Riggs and Plano (1994: 56-57) explains, this procedure of simple majority vote – as opposed to a two-third majority vote used in "important questions" involving international peace and security – has evolved into a "consensus approach to decision making," which is the procedure of "*adoption without vote*." The procedure of adoption without vote was used for the adoption of the two programs, which were adopted without any possibility of rejection.

This procedure was flawed because it allowed any group of countries to have the UN General Assembly adopt almost any kind of resolution, as long as this group has enough support to impose its agenda. This was obviously the case in the adoption of UNPAAERD and UNNADAF, which were imposed by the group of African countries with a strong support from the Group of 77 and the Non-Aligned Movement. As a result, the UN General Assembly adopted these two development programs, even though they were poorly designed and potentially ineffective, and some member states were reasonably opposed to their adoption.

Inappropriate Processes of Implementation and Evaluation

Despite the flaws in the processes of formulation, recommendation, and adoption of UNPAAERD and UNNADAF, one may still argue that if these two UN development programs were fully implemented, they could have somewhat improved the economic and social conditions of Africa, or at least, that they could have increased the level of self-reliance and self-sufficiency in agricultural and industrial production on the continent. However, as we have seen in Chapters 2 and 3, the implementation of these two UN development programs was seriously handicapped by the non-compliance of both the African countries themselves and the international community. This resulted in the lack of policy actions (i.e., inputs and processes) necessary for their full implementation. Besides, because of the flaws in their formulation, no specific administrator (individual or organization) was designated to be directly in charge of their implementation. Furthermore, the two UN development programs were not rigorously evaluated and the same mistakes were repeated over and over.

Concerning the policy inputs (i.e., money, time, personnel, equipment and any other required resources), the implementation of the two UN development programs was not based on the regular budget of the UN organization nor on that of any UN agencies (UNDP or UNIDO, for instance), but on the voluntary contributions by member states. As a result, the financial resources and the personnel required for the implementation of the two programs were not available at the time of their adoption. As demonstrated in Chapters 2 and 3 demonstrated, the required financial resources did not come forth as expected. In the case of UNPAAERD, not only were the African countries unable to mobilize the required $82.5 billion in domestic resources, but their domestic savings and investment were actually declining during the period of the implementation of this program.[11] In the case of UNNADAF, the capitalist developed countries could not provide the required $30 billion in net ODA, nor were they able to increase their financial assistance to Africa at the average rate of 4 per cent a year. In fact, the flows of ODA to Africa were declining at the dramatic rate of 17.2 per cent a year during the period of the implementation of UNNADAF (1990-1999).[12] Because of this lack of policy inputs, the implementation of the two UN development programs did not in reality take place.

In application of the concept of *global compact*, everybody (each African country and each member of the international community) was responsible for the implementation of the two programs. However, since no specific entity was designated to administer the two programs, nobody appeared in fact to be directly responsible for their implementation. This lack of specific administrator also constituted one of the major obstacles for the full implementation of the two UN development programs. As the final review of UNPAAERD puts it:

> The Programme of Action itself was silent regarding who was to act if unforeseen exogenous contingencies threw the Programme of Action off course; also, its review machinery did not clearly address this issue. (UN document No. A/RES/46/151 of 18 December, annex II.A, parag. 2)

As mentioned earlier, different structures have been used, under UNNADAF, to remedy this lack of administrator, such as the Office of the Special Coordinator for Africa and the Least Developed Countries, and the Inter-agency Task Force for the Implementation of the UNNADAF. However, none of these entities could successfully play the role of program administrator. Thus, as the final review of UNPAAERD correctly put it: "the concept of global compact at the continental level was difficult to achieve."[13]

Finally, as mentioned earlier, the two UN development programs did not become the general frameworks for assistance to Africa. Instead of complying to the provisions of these programs, the capitalist developed countries and the Bretton Woods institutions, which controlled the bulk of the ODA for Africa, continued to support the SAPs. During the 1980s and 1990s, almost all forms of financial assistance from the capitalist developed countries and the Bretton Woods institutions to any individual African country were conditioned by the adoption of SAPs by that country. In addition, even the UNDP, which was supposed to be more compliant with the decisions of the UN General Assembly, did not refer to the two UN development programs as the frameworks for its assistance to individual African countries. Instead, it continued to use its "round-table discussions" in providing assistance to those countries.[14] Consequently, nobody was actually implementing the two UN development programs, and nothing was done to change this situation.

With regard to the process of evaluation, the UN General Assembly did not evaluate rigorously and objectively these two development programs. Almost all of the mistakes made in the formulation and implementation of the first development program (UNPAAERD) were repeated in the formulation and implementation of the second one (UNNADAF). Indeed, while everyone (including the

UN Secretary-General) who reviewed UNPAAERD, concluded that this program failed to achieve its objectives, the UN General Assembly refused to admit this failure, and found a way to argue that it was "far from being a failure." This inaccurate evaluation clearly indicates that the UN General Assembly was poised to repeat the same mistakes made in the formulation and implementation of this first program in those of the second program (UNNADAF). Furthermore, the mid-term evaluation of this second program did not result in any improvement of its implementation.

In sum, among the major mistakes made in the formulation and implementation of the two UN development programs, we can point to the fact that both programs were based on the same concept of *global compact* and had the same goal and strategy of *collective self-reliance.* Furthermore, both programs suffered from the non-compliance of almost all parties involved and from the lack of specific administrator directly in charge of their implementation.

Conclusion

The application of structuralist theory and/or dependency theory in interpreting the causes of the critical economic and social conditions in Africa in the 1980s and 1990s led the group of African countries to identify wrong problems and prescribe inappropriate solutions through UNPAAERD and UNNADAF.   In applying these theories in the context of Africa, this group drew the conclusion that the most important obstacles to economic and social development on the continent were the "lack of structural transformation" (i.e., lack of industrialization) of the African economies, their dependence of on the world   economy,   and   their   vulnerability   to   external   shocks. Consequently, instead of addressing directly the most crucial problems of Africa (such as armed conflicts, political instability, lack of good governance, economic mismanagement, droughts and deterioration of the environment), the two UN development programs, which have been strongly influenced by the group of African countries, were specifically designed to solve these so-called problems of structural transformation, dependence, and vulnerability of the African economies. The solutions prescribed by these programs were rooted in the unrealistic goal and strategy of *collective self-reliance.*   Under   the   first   program (UNPAAERD), these solutions included, among other things, the development of agriculture and the sectors in support of the agriculture;

and under the second program (UNNADAF), they included the promotion of import-substituting industrialization (ISI), along with the development of regional cooperation and integration.

The flaws in the processes of policy recommendation and adoption within the UN General Assembly allowed the adoption of these programs, even though they were potentially ineffective and some member states were actually opposed to their adoption. This was because the only criterion used in their recommendation was their responsiveness to the African priorities. Besides, the procedure of *adoption without vote* was also used for their adoption by the UN General Assembly.

Moreover, the implementation of the two UN development programs was seriously handicapped by the lack of policy actions (i.e., inputs and processes). The required financial resources did not come forth as expected, no specific entity was designated to administer them, and almost all member states and all international organizations did not fully comply with their provisions. As a result, the implementation of these two UN development programs did not even take place.

Finally, the UN General Assembly did not rigorously nor accurately evaluate these two programs. As a result, each evaluation did not lead to the identification of the most important causes of failure, and did not contribute to any improvement. Consequently, the same mistakes were made in both of these programs.

Notes

[1] UN document No. A/AC.229/2* of 23 April 1986, p. 7, parag. 14; and UN document No. A/46/280 of 2 July 1991, p. 15, parag. 66.3.

[2] UN document No. A/S-11/14 of 21 August 1980, annex I.

[3] UN document No. A/44/315 of 21 June 1989, annex; or UN document No. E/ECA/CM.15/6/Rev.3.

[4] UN document No. A/44/315 of 21 June 1989, annex, p. 25, parag. 72.

[5] This concept was launched by the United Nations Children's Fund (UNICEF) in 1985 in its report entitled *Within Human Reach: A Future for Africa's Children, The Prospect*, which mainly argues that, because of their focuses on macroeconomic indicators, the social consequences of the SAPs for the

vulnerable social groups in Africa (women and children) were dramatic. The International Conference on the Human Dimension of Africa's Recovery an Development, held in Khartoom (Sudan) in March 1988, translated this concept into a "human-focused approach to socio-economic recovery and development" (UN document No. A/43/430 of 29 June 1988, annex I).

[6] The rivalry between the two organizations was demonstrated by the consistent attack of the World Bank's structural adjustment programs by the UNDP in its different issues of *Human Development Report*. As a matter of fact, the *African Alternative Framework to Structural Adjustment Programmes (AAF-SAP)* was sponsored by the UNDP.

[7] As we noted in Chapter 3, Section 3.2.1, the final review of UNPAAERD recognized that two thirds of the African countries that pursued structural adjustment policies, received increased international assistance, and achieved "modest gains" in per capita income, while the countries that did not undertake structural adjustment, continued to decline (UN document No. A/RES/41/151 of 18 December 1991, Annex I.A., parag. 10).

[8] See the case of Madagascar, in Chapter 6, below.

[9] UN document No. A/RES/40/40 of 02 December 1985, parag. 4.

[10] *Charter of the United Nations*, Article 18.3.

[11] See Table 2.2 – Implementation of UNPAAERD: Available Financial Resources, above, chapter 2, p. 29.

[12] See Table 3.2 – Implementation of UNNADAF: Available Financial Resources, above, chapter 3, p. 55.

[13] UN document No. A/RES/46/151 of 18 December, annex II.B.2(B), parag. 2.

[14] *Ibid.*.

Chapter 5

The External Causes of the Failure of UNPAAERD and UNNADAF

The external causes of the failure UNPAAERD and UNNADAF were related to the late 20th century world economic order,[1] which exercised powerful constraints upon the implementation of these UN development programs and ultimately led to their failure. The UN actions in development, as reflected in UNPAAERD and UNNADAF, didn't have any chance to succeed within this particular world economic order.

Using Robert Cox's "framework for action" or "historical structure" to picture and investigate the interacting forces within the late 20th century world economic order, this chapter analyzes how the two UN development programs responded to the constraints imposed by these forces, which were constituted by capitalist material capabilities, liberal ideas, and the Bretton Woods institutions.

The Constraints Imposed by the Late 20th Century Capitalist Material Capabilities

As mentioned earlier, *material capabilities* can be simply defined as "productive and destructive potentials," which exist in their dynamic form as "technological and organizational capabilities"; and in their accumulated form as "natural resources which technology can transform, stocks of equipment (for example, industries and armaments), and the wealth which can command these" (Cox, 1986: 218). Within the late 20th century world economic order, the dominant material capabilities were based on capitalism, which completely transformed the world since its origins in Europe in the 15th-16th centuries, and which was at the origin of the modern world economy, and the phenomenon of globalization (Wood, 1999; Polanyi, 1944).

Generally speaking, capitalism is "a social and economic system in which individuals are free to own the means of production and maximize profits and in which resource allocation is determined by the price system" (Bannock, G. et al.. Eds., 1987: 64-65). Since its origins, capitalism had different forms and evolved across time and space. However, despite these different forms, it was fundamentally characterized by:

1. Private ownership of property,
2. No legal limit on the accumulation of property,
3. The free market – no [or reduced] government intervention in the economy,
4. The profit motive as the driving force of [the economic activities], and
5. Profit as the measure of efficiency. (Sargent, 1993: 82)

According to Robert Cox (1987), two basic forms of capitalism coexisted in the late 20th century:

- A competitive capitalism of small or medium businesses at the national level, and
- A monopoly capitalism of multinational corporations (MNCs) or transnational corporations (TNCs) at the international level.

It is this second form of capitalism that is very important in understanding the power of capitalism and the domination of capitalist material capabilities of the late 20th century. As other analysts, such as Richard Barnet and John Cavanagh, point out, these MNCs or TNCs were increasingly controlling "the human energy, capital, and technology that are making [the *world economy*] happen" (Barnet and Cavanagh, 1994: 14-15).

Describing the characteristics of the late 20th century world economy, Robert Cox (1987) observes that it consisted of "transnational production organizations" whose component elements were located in different territorial jurisdictions. In connection with this, the author notes that:

> Each of these transnational production organizations produces for the world market. Each takes advantage of differences in costs and

availabilities of factors of production in deciding about the location of its component elements.

Knowledge, in the form of technology and market information, is the principal resource in the world economy, especially knowledge in its dynamic form as the capacity to generate new technologies and to market new products. Money can be tapped where it is to be found by those who have the knowledge assets, e.g., in local capital markets or in international credit. (Cox, 1987: 244)

In other words, the capitalist material capabilities in the late 20th century world economic order was made up of "technological and organizational capabilities" generated by capitalism and characterized by:

- The domination of MNCs, which controlled human energy, capital and technology, and produced for the world market,
- The importance of knowledge, in the form of technology and market information, as the principal resource,
- The availability of money in domestic and international markets for those who have the knowledge assets, and
- The phenomenon of globalization.

The mere existence of these capitalist material capabilities, which gave enormous economic and military power to the capitalist developed countries, constrained the less developed countries (LDCs) to embrace the capitalist system, open their economies to international trade and investment, reduce the role of the state or public sector in their economies, and adopt an outward-looking development strategy (Rapley, 1996; Cox, 1987). There are two main reasons why they had to follow these constraints.

First, as Kenneth Waltz (1999) points out, in a competitive system like the world economy in the late 20th century, the losers (i.e., the LDCs) had no choice but to imitate the winners (i.e., the capitalist developed countries). Otherwise, they would continue to loose. Moreover, the author also argues that the "end of the Cold War and the collapse of communism have discredited all models other than [the capitalist model of development]" (Waltz, 1999).

Second, the LDCs may choose to defy the constraints imposed by the capitalist material capabilities. However, in doing so they would have to pay heavy prices, which may include the difficulty (if not impossibility) of buying and selling anything on the world market, securing domestic and foreign investment, and benefiting from advanced technologies (Waltz, 1999; Cox, 1987). As Kenneth Waltz (1999) also points out, only a few oil-rich countries could afford to pay such prices. The other countries (particularly Cuba and North Korea), which chose to do so because of their ideological conviction had to endure the disastrous consequences of the marginalization of their economies from the world economy.

In response to the constraints imposed by the capitalist material capabilities, the designers of UNPAAERD and UNNADAF clearly chose to defy them by prescribing measures related to a state-run economic system and an inward-looking development strategy based on the concept of *collective self-reliance*. There was no place for capitalism, MNCs and FDI in this state-run economic system and this inward-looking development strategy. As mentioned earlier, the two UN development programs were actually designed to solve the so-called problems of capitalist domination and exploitation, along with their consequences (i.e., the dependence of the African economies and their vulnerability to external shocks).

Therefore, even the most fundamental characteristics of capitalism (such as private ownership of property, free market, and profit motive) were ignored under these two UN development programs. Instead, their full implementation would have promoted an economic system in which the state and the public sectors would be the main economic actors, and in which there would be no (or little) place for private ownership of property, free market, and profit motive. This was clearly stated in Resolution S-13/2, which stipulated that the implementation of UNPAAERD was based on the assumption that "the public sector will have to continue to play an important role in the development of the region."[2] With regard to UNNADAF, its implementation, as described in the *African Alternative Framework to the Structural Adjustment Program* (*AAF-SAP*), would require each African state to set up a centrally planned economy in which only the "vital goods and services" would be taken into consideration and the "category of luxuries and semi-luxuries" would be discarded.[3]

Furthermore, the group of African countries, which influenced the formulation of the two UN development programs, clearly intended to close the African economies to MNCs and FDI, and to limit the participation of African countries in the world economy. These measures were based on the assumption that the "openness and excessive dependence" of the African economies to the world economy would have constituted the "most fundamental causes of [the] underdevelopment and retrogression" of Africa.[4] Therefore, the group of African countries adopted the goal and strategy of *collective self-reliance*, so that each African country would have only to produce for the national and regional market, instead of producing for the world market. In addition, the two UN development programs promoted regional and subregional cooperation and integration, which were expected to "bring about an effective transformation" of the African economies.[5] They also promoted South-South cooperation as the "key element in the economic recovery of Africa,"[6] or as an "indispensable element for the success."[7]

Finally, the African goal and strategy of *collective self-reliance* also required the adoption of an inward-looking development strategy, as opposed to the outward-looking development strategy imposed by the capitalist material capabilities. As mentioned earlier, this inward-looking development strategy was based on the development of the agriculture and the sectors in support of the agriculture under UNPAAERD, and on the promotion of import-substituting industrialization (ISI), and regional cooperation and integration under UNNADAF.

However, it turned out that no African country was able to fully implement the two UN development programs. In fact, if any of them had tried to do so, it would have had to pay the heavy prices mentioned earlier. In other words, if Africa as a whole persisted in fully implementing these two UN development programs, its already advanced state of marginalization would have been aggravated, its share of the world output would have continued to decline, and nobody would have invested in Africa "except in narrowly defined mineral enclave sectors" such as the oil refineries in Nigeria or Angola (Callaghy, 1995: 42).

Faced with such prospect, most African countries actually had no other choice than to follow the constraints imposed by the capitalist material capabilities, which led them to embrace capitalism, open up their economy to MNCs and FDI, and adopt an outward-looking development strategy. All of these measures were included in the SAPs sponsored by the Bretton Woods institutions and the capitalist developed countries. As a result, the adoption of the SAPs automatically compelled most African countries to abandon the full implementation of the two UN development programs.

The Constraints Imposed by the Late 20th Century Liberal Ideas

In his definition of *ideas,* as one of the three interacting forces within a framework of action or historical structure, Robert Cox (1986) distinguishes, on the one hand, "intersubjective meanings" or "shared notions of the nature of social relations which tend to perpetuate habits and expectations of behavior" (Cox, 1986: 218-219); and, on the other hand, "collective images of social order held by different groups of people" (Cox, 1986: 218-219).

The dominant ideas which perpetuated "habits and expectations" within the late 20th century world economic order were clearly the *liberal ideas,* which were related to capitalism and democracy. These ideas were so dominant that some analysts simply describe the late 20th century world economic order as a "liberal international order" (Barnett, 1997).

The concept of *"liberal ideas"* or *"liberalism"* (under which different types of liberal ideas can be put together) is difficult to define and can be confusing and misleading at times (Baldwin, 1993). This is because *liberalism,* like capitalism, has changed through time and space, and does not always mean the same thing from one century to another, or from one country to another. As *Encyclopedia Britanica* puts it nicely, "liberalism is the creed of those who believe in individual liberty.   More specifically, since 'no government allows absolute liberty,' it is the belief that it is desirable to maximize the amount of liberty in the state" ("Liberalism," 1994-1999).

Furthermore, what is known as the *classical liberalism* of the 18th and 19th centuries was based on the "sovereignty of the market," the "natural harmony of interests," and the "self-adjusting market mechanism," which were developed by classical liberal theorists such as Adam Smith.   According to these ideas, "if individuals are left free to pursue their self-interest in an exchange economy based upon a division of labour, the welfare of the group as a whole will necessary be enhanced" ("Liberalism," 1994-1999).   Consequently, classical liberal theorists generally argue that not only should the power of the state be limited, but also that the state should not interfere with the economic life of the community ("Liberalism," 1994-1999).

In the aftermath of World War II, the so-called "Keynesian consensus" emerged and was applied by most capitalist countries around the world.   Based on the economic theory of John M. Keynes, this consensus allowed some forms of government intervention in the economy. This is why some analysts, like Robert Cox, describe the "Keynesian consensus" as "neoliberalism." In this sense, John Rapley (1996) notes that John M. Keynes advocated the "use of fiscal policy" or government spending to deal with recession. Thus, "by building roads and dams, for example, a government could create jobs, which in turn could create more demand for goods and services, which would cause factories to increase their output and then to take on more workers, and so on in an upward spiral" (Rapley, 1996:   8-9). Furthermore, the author mentions that the "Keynesian consensus" was also characterized by the consensus on the protection of vulnerable social groups through welfare programs.

As a result of the economic recessions of the 1970s, however, the Keynesian consensus quickly faded away in most capitalist developed countries (Spero and Hart, 1997; Rapley, 1996; Cox, 1987). While some analysts argue that there was a return to the *classical liberal ideas* of the 18th and 19th centuries in many capitalist developed countries (Rapley, 1996; Sargent, 1993), other analysts, like Robert Cox (1987), contend that there were, in fact, two competing variants of *liberal ideas* in the 1980s and 1990s: (1) the *hyperliberal ideas* found in Reaganism in the United States and in Thatcherism in Great Britain, and (2) the *state-capitalist ideas* held by social-democrats in other capitalist developed countries, particularly in West Germany and Japan.

Robert Cox (1987) describes the *hyperliberal ideas* in Reaganism and Thatcherism as an "anticipation of a hyperliberal form of state." According to the author, these ideas revived the 19th century economic liberalism, and rejected the "neoliberal attempt to adapt economic liberalism to the socio-political reactions that classical liberalism produced" (Cox, 1987: 286-287). As he puts it:

> The whole paraphernalia of Keynesian demand-support and redis-tributionist tools of policy are regarded with the deepest suspicion in the hyperliberal approach. Government spending to create employment, and the transfer payments to targeted groups intended to sustain their purchasing power and thus indirectly to maintain employment, fall under this suspicion. So also do other kinds of government intervention to support industries in difficulty such as credits, bailouts, price supports, and subsidies [...]. (Cox, 1987: 286-287)

These *hyperliberal ideas* prescribed, among other things, respect for the sovereignty of the market economy, reduction of government intervention in the economy, reduction of the government spending, an end to welfare programs at the national level, and an end to development assistance to developing countries at the international level.

With regard to *state-capitalist ideas*, Robert Cox notes that these ideas took different forms according to "national positions within the world economy and by institutional structures and ideologies" (Cox, 1987: 290). He argues, however, that the substance common to these different forms consisted in "a recognition of the indispensable *guiding role of the state* in the development of the nation's productive forces and the advancement of their position in the world economy through the mediation of the state in a corporative process" (Cox, 1987: 290) (Emphasis added). According to the author, the *state-capitalist ideas* may have produced in different states some kind of agreement among different social groups on the "strategic goals of the economy" and also on the "sharing of burdens and benefits in the effort to reach those goals."

Moreover, Robert Cox argues that the *state-capitalist ideas* were also grounded in the belief that the "world market" was the "ultimate determinant of development." As he puts it:

> States are assumed to intervene not only to enhance the competitiveness of their nations' industries but also to negotiate or dictate advantages for their nations' exporters. The world market is the state of nature from which state-capitalist theory deduces specific policy. (Cox, 1987: 290)

Furthermore, Robert Cox notes that the development policy derived from the *state-capitalist ideas* included the "development of the leading sectors of national production so as to give them a competitive edge in world markets," and the "protection of the principal social groups so that their welfare can be perceived as linked to the success of the national productive effort" (Cox, 1987: 290).

In other words, the *state-capitalist ideas* preserved some elements of the Keynesian consensus, particularly the idea that the government should intervene to some extent in the economy, and protect the vulnerable social groups. However, the main difference between these *state-capitalist ideas* and the Keynesian consensus concerned the role of the state in the world economy. Contrary to the Keynesian consensus, *state-capitalist ideas* emphasized the so-called "*guiding role of the state*" in the world economy.

Liberal ideas helped capitalism to flourish since the 18th centuries and to produce the awesome capitalist material capabilities in the late 20th century. Since these ideas were the origin of the enormous economic and military power to the capitalist developed countries, they also compelled the LDCs to follow their prescriptions, which included protection of individual freedom and individual entrepreneurship, respect for the sovereignty of the market, and reduction of the role of state and the public sector in the economy.

The two reasons that explained why the LDCs had to follow the constraints imposed by the capitalist material capabilities can be also used here to explain why these countries had to follow the constraints of the liberal ideas. These reasons were: on the one hand, in the competitive system of the late 20th century, the losers (i.e., LDCs) had to imitate the winners (i.e., capitalist developed countries), or they would continue to lose; and on the other hand, if the losers decided not to imitate the winners, they would have to pay heavy prices (Waltz, 1999). In addition to these two reasons, the end of the Cold War and the total collapse of communism at the end of the 1980s have completely discredited all other ideas, except the liberal ideas held by the capitalist developed countries. Consequently, the LDCs had no other alternatives than the liberal ideas and the capitalist system.

Despite these constraints imposed by the liberal ideas of the late 20th century world economic order, UNPAAERD and UNNADAF were in essence formulated to defy them. In this sense, these two UN development programs promoted some *collectivist ideas* based on the concept of *collective self-reliance*. Thus, instead of following the constraints of the liberal ideas, these programs prescribed different measures that included mass mobilization, economic redistribution, and unlimited intervention of the state and the public sector in the economy.

Moreover, instead of promoting and protecting individual freedom and individual entrepreneurship they emphasized collectivism at the national and regional levels. Indeed, looming behind the concept of *collective self-reliance* contained in the two UN development programs were the ideas that the African countries would have to "rely exclusively on internal means of stimulating and coordinating the productive forces in [their] society" (Cox, 1987: 306). According to Robert Cox, this would mean "mobilization, collective and egalitarian austerity, and the organization of production geared to use (or the basic needs of society) rather than exchange (or the possibility of profits on world market)," and would also imply "a shift, not toward the defensive-protectionist strategy, but toward the construction of a redistributive system" (Cox, 1987: 306).

Furthermore, instead of respecting the "sovereignty of the market economy," the two UN development programs sought to set up a redistributive economic system in which the state would have to determine the "vital goods and services" to be taken into consideration, and the "category of luxuries and semi-luxuries" to be discarded.[8] In other words, even if the African policy makers did not explicitly recommend the establishment of a redistributive or socialist system, the implementation of the two UN development programs would have logically led to the establishment of such a system.

Finally, since the two UN development programs were based on the idea that the state and the public sector would remain the main economic actors in Africa, there was no intention to reduce the roles of these entities in the two UN development programs. In fact, in the case of UNNADAF, each African state would have to set up a centrally planned economy in which the state would have to determine the type of goods and services to be produced.[9]

In sum, UNPAAERD and UNNADAF were in essence designed to defy the constraints imposed by the liberal ideas of the late 20th century world economic order. Consequently, their full implementation would have constituted a serious threat to individual freedom, individual entrepreneurship, and market economy in Africa.

However, any African country that would have tried to fully implement these two UN development programs based on collectivist ideas would have also to pay the prices, which would have included flight of capital, disinvestments, and decline of ODA and FDI. Indeed, the private companies and individuals who were already investing in the country, would have felt that their investments were no longer secure, and would have chosen to move them to other countries. In addition, new investors would not be attracted to the country because of the threats to individual freedom, individual entrepreneurship and market economy contained in those programs. Even the ODA from the capitalist developed countries and the Bretton Woods institutions would have declined as a result of the implementation of these programs.

For illustrative purposes, we may refer to the particular case of Madagascar.[10] In 1975-1976, the government of that country, putting into practice its socialist ideas based on "autonomous development" and "self-sufficiency," decided to nationalize all major private companies implanted in the country. One of the immediate consquences of this nationalization was that the FDI to the country, which averaged $11 million a year at the beginning of the 1970s, turned into a flight of capital, averaging $3 million a year over the period of 1977-1979 (World Bank, 1993: 390-391). In addition, the ODA from the capitalist developed countries dropped, in current prices, from an annual average of $65 million in 1973-1975 to an annual average of $33 million in 1977-1978 (OECD, 1978, 1979/1982). It was only in 1989, three years after the implementation of the first SAP with the Bretton Woods institutions, that the country could once again attract FDI (World Bank, 1993: 390-391). And by this time, the ODA from the capitalist developed countries jumped to an annual average of $326 million (OECD, 1989/1992).

Facing the prospects of capital flight, disinvestment, and decline of ODA and FDI, any responsible African government had to abandon the collectivist ideas put forward by UNPAAERD and UNNADAF. This is why most African political leaders had in fact to embrace the liberal ideas promoted by the Bretton Woods institutions and the capitalist developed countries through the SAPs. In reality, the vague commitment to improve human rights and to intensify the democratization process mentioned in the two UN development programs (particularly in UNNADAF) were not enough to ensure the national and international investors, as well as the international donors.

In sum, the dominant liberal ideas of the late 20th century forced most international actors to respect the basic principles of capitalism and democracy. The constraints imposed by these liberal ideas also explain the abandonment of the two UN development programs by the African countries, which could not fully implement without enduring disastrous economic consequences within the late 20th century world economic order.

The Constraints Imposed by the Bretton Woods Institutions

As Robert Cox puts it, *institutions* are "particular amalgams of ideas and material power which in turn influence the development of ideas and material capabilities" (Cox, 1986: 219). The author also states that: "institutionalization is a means of stabilizing and perpetuating a particular order" (Cox, 1986: 219).

In the late 20th century, the dominant international institutions, which interacted with the capitalist material capabilities and the liberal ideas, and tended to stabilize and perpetuate the world economy order, were certainly the Bretton Woods institutions, which were constituted by the combination of the International Monetary Fund (IMF) and the World Bank. These institutions, supported by the capitalist material capabilities and guided by the liberal ideas of the late 20th century, exercised powerful constraints on the members of the international community, particularly on the African countries and the UN.

Describing its main function, the IMF recently restates that:

> A main function of the IMF is to provide loans to countries experiencing balance-of-payments problems so that they can restore conditions for sustainable economic growth. The financial assistance provided by the IMF enables countries to rebuild their international reserves, stabilize their currencies, and continue paying for imports without having to impose trade restrictions or capital controls. Unlike development banks, the IMF does not lend for specific projects. (International Monetaty Fund, 2002)

Many analysts, particularly Narisoa Rajaonarivony (1996) in the case of Madagascar, point out that it was this important function, as the "lender of the last resort," which gave the IMF and additionally the World Bank their tremendous power in the world economy. Robert Cox (1987) equates this function as a certification of the "creditworthiness" (or credibility) of the "economically weakened countries" (Cox, 1987: 255). Without such certification it would be difficult (if not impossible) for any country to do business on the world market, especially to borrow money either from any other international financial institution or from any other country.

Another important role of the Bretton Woods institutions was to make sure that the international financial system functioned properly and that all international actors played by the rules. This is what Robert Cox (1987) describes as the "system maintenance and supervisory role" of the Bretton Woods institutions. While many analysts have been speculating about the so-called "breakdown of Bretton Woods system" (Spero and Hart, 1997: 16-24), the fact was that the roles and functions of the IMF and the World Bank as "lenders of last resort," guarantors of the creditworthiness of economically weakened countries, and "supervisors" of the international financial system have not changed that much. On the contrary, these roles and functions have been strengthened since the 1980s (Cox, 1987: 302). This was particularly true with regard to the African countries, whose ability to borrow on the international financial market completely depended on the Bretton Woods institutions.

These different roles and functions of the Bretton Woods institutions, which gave them a tremendous power in the late 20th century world economic order, allowed them to force almost any country in the world (with the exception of the United States and few other capitalist developed countries) to follow their prescriptions. In the case of the African countries and most LDCs, the prescriptions of the Bretton Woods institutions usually took the form of "structural adjustment programs" (SAPs). These programs had different forms, depending on the country and time period where they were implemented. However, according to most analysts the most important measures commonly included in a typical SAP were:

- *Macroeconomic stabilization*, which is aimed at returning or maintaining the economy of the debtor country to an equilibrium, and may include reduction of budget deficit or deduction of trade deficit,
- *Price liberalization*, which involves "need for market prices to reflect relative scarcities," as opposed to price control, and
- *Revision of the role of state and the public sector*, which may include reduction of the role of the state and the public sector in the economy, privatization of state-own enterprises, etc.

The consequences of ignoring or violating the prescriptions of the Bretton Woods institutions could be disastrous, not only for LDCs like those in Africa, but also for most capitalist developed countries. These consequences involved, among other things, flight of capital, disinvestments, and difficulty to do business on the international financial market. In connection with this, Robert Cox (1987) refers to the cases of Great Britain and France in the 1970s and 1980s to show the dramatic economic and social consequences of ignoring the Bretton Woods institutions' prescriptions, and to demonstrate the power of these institutions in constraining these countries.[11]

Most African countries were well aware of the power of the Bretton Woods institutions and the consequences of ignoring their prescriptions. It was in this sense that the ECA noted in the *African Alternative Framework to Structural Adjustment Programmes (AAF-SAP)* that: "Many African countries have had to adopt IMF and World Bank-supported stabilization and structural adjustment programmes to obtain emergency balance of payments assistance and badly-needed external finance."[12] Indeed, only the Bretton Woods institutions had the ultimate solutions for these problems of balance of payments and external debt. The UN, expected by the group of African countries to solve these problems, did not have the means, nor the power to do so.

Other consequences of ignoring the Bretton Woods institutions' prescriptions would also include decline in ODA and FDI. As we will see in the cases of Madagascar and Mauritius,[13] there was an alliance between the Bretton Woods institutions, the capitalist developed countries, and the MNCs, so that the flows of ODA and FDI to developing countries were generally conditioned by their agreements with the Bretton Woods institutions. In other words, if a given LDC was experiencing severe problems of balance of payments and external debt, it had first to reach an agreement with the Bretton Woods institutions, before the capitalist developed countries and the MNCs decided to provide ODA and FDI.

UNPAAERD and UNNADAF contained some of the prescriptions of the Bretton Woods institutions, which were described as "policy reforms" in the two programs, and comprised such measures as "marcoeconomic adjustment" in UNPAAERD, and "improvement of domestic economic management" in UNNADAF. However, not only were these measures adopted for political expediency, but they were not the priorities of the two UN development programs. In fact, some measures contained in the two UN development programs were clearly in contradiction with these prescriptions of the Bretton Woods institutions.

As we have pointed out earlier, one of the major guidelines of the two UN development programs consisted in making the state and the public sector the major economic actors in Africa. This was clearly stipulated in Resolution S-13/2, annex II, with regard to UNPAAERD,[14] and in the *African Alternative Framework to the Structural Adjustment Program (AAF-SAP)*, in the case of UNNADAF.[15] In this sense, the full implementation of these two programs by any African country would have led that country to violate one of the most important prescriptions of the Bretton Woods institutions on the reduction of the role of the state and the public sector in the economy and the privatization of state-owned enterprises. As a result of such violation, the African country in question would have had to face the sanctions imposed by the Bretton Woods institutions.

No responsible African political leader would want his/her country to endure these sanctions. As a result, most of them had no choice but to follow the prescriptions of the Bretton Woods institutions, and automatically abandon the implementation of the two UN development programs. Thus, these programs had no chance to be successfully implemented within the late 20th century world economic order dominated by the Bretton Woods institutions.

Conclusion

The constraints imposed by the interacting forces within the late 20th century world economic order (capitalist material capabilities, variants of liberal ideas and the Bretton Woods institutions) did not give UNPAAERD and UNNADAF any chance to succeed, and decisively contributed to their failure. First, the constraints imposed by the capitalist material capabilities compelled most African countries to embrace capitalism, open up their economy to international trade and FDI, and adopt an outward-looking strategy in order to avoid further economic instability and marginalization from the world economy. By adhering to these constraints they were automatically compelled to abandon the two UN development programs, which prescribed a distributive economic system and an inward-looking development strategy based on the concept of collective self-reliance.

Second, the domination of liberal ideas in the late 20th century also forced the African countries to embrace the basic elements of liberalism associated with capitalism and democracy, including individual freedom, individual entrepreneurship, sovereignty of the market, and reduced role of the state and the public sector. The adoption of these liberal ideas also compelled the African countries to abandon the two UN development programs, which promoted different ideas related to collectivism, distributive economic system, and substantial state intervention in the economy.

Finally, the powerful constraints imposed by the Bretton Woods institutions decisively compelled the African countries to adopt structural adjustment programs (SAPs), which included macro-economic stabilization, price liberalization, and reduced role of the state and the public sector. The adoption of these measures related to the SAPs led them also to abandon the two UN development programs, which did not help them to borrow money from the international financial market, and get more ODA and FDI.

Notes

[1] As mentioned earlier, our conception of "world economic order" is based on Robert Cox's definition of "world orders" as "particular configurations of forces which successively define the problematic of war or peace for the ensemble of states" (Cox, 1986: 220).

[2] UN document No. A/RES/S-13/2 of 01 June 1986, Annex II.A.1(e).(i).

[3] UN document No. A/44/315 of 21 June 1989, p. 27, parag. 76.

[4] UN document No. A/44/315 of 21 June 1989, p. 2, parag. 5.

[5] UN document No. A/RES/46/151 of 18 December 1991, Annex II.B.1(b), parag. 11.

[6] UN document No. A/RES/S-13/2 of 01 June 1986, Annex II.B, parag. 18.

[7] UN document No. A/RES/46/151 of 18 December 1991, Annex II.B.1(i), parag. 20.

[8] UN document No. A/44/315 of 21 June 1989, p. 27, parag. 76.

[9] UN document No. A/44/315 of 21 June 1989, p. 27, parag. 76.

[10] See Chapter 6, below.

[11] With regard to Great Britain, Robert Cox (1987: 306) noted that the British Labour government was forced in 1976 to reduce state expenditures as a proportion of GNP by a combination of IMF pressures and the high cost of borrowing in the domestic finance market. And regarding France, Robert Cox reported that the French Socialist government under President Francois Mitterand ignored the rules of the international financial system, and had to face deficits in the social services and unemployment insurance, in public and private enterprises, and in the balance of payments of the country. As a result, it was forced to align its policies on those of the other developed capitalist countries.

[12] UN document No. A/44/315 of 21 June 1989, Annex, p. 20, parag. 61.

[13] See Chapters 6 and 7, below.

[14] UN document No. A/RES/S-13/2 of 01 June 1986, Annex II.A.1(e).(i).

[15] UN document No. A/RES/46/151 of 18 December 1991, Annex II.B.1(a).

Chapter 6

The Case of Madagascar

When Madagascar received its independence from France, its former colonial power, on June 26, 1960, it seemed to have what would take to develop: abundant natural resources, and a relatively well-educated elite and workforce (Serpa, 1991). In addition, compared to many other African countries, the island did not suffer from protracted armed conflicts, nor did it suffer from severe deterioration of the environment or permanent droughts, which have provoked famine and hunger on the continent. Furthermore, although the political leaders of the country were not always successful, they seemed to care about the welfare of the *Malagasy*[1] people, and tried different types of development strategies and programs.

However, despite these advantages, Madagascar can be considered a case of failed development. Instead of becoming one of the most advanced countries in Africa, it is now classified among the 10 poorest countries in the world, with a per capita GNP of $250 and a life expectancy at birth of 58 (World Bank, 2001; Thomas, 1998; Serpa, 1991).

This chapter discusses the case of Madagascar within the context of UNPAAERD and UNNADAF, and explains why these programs could not help solving the economic and social problems of this country in the 1980s and 1990s. In doing so, it will first present a general background about this country. Next, referring to each UN development program, it will define its economic and social problems, present the solutions adopted by its government, and demonstrate how and why each one of the UN development programs failed to address these problems.

General Background About Madagascar

Madagascar, the fourth largest island in the world, lies about 210 miles (390 kilometers) from the East coast of Africa, across the Mozambique Channel. It extends 863 miles (1,600 kilometers) from North to South, and up to 307 miles (570 kilometers) from East to West. The whole territory covers an area of 226,658 square miles (587,041 square kilometers) (Thompson, 1997).

The inhabitants of the island, traditionally divided into 18 ethnic groups, are the descendants of successive waves of immigrants from East Africa, Arabia, and South-East Asia. The first waves of immigrants from South-East Asia are believed to have reached the island some 2000 years ago. Other groups, from the African continent and the Arab peninsula, came later on. Two major ethnic groups, the *Merina* and the *Betsileo*, mostly of South-East Asian origin, inhabit the central highlands (or the *plateaux*). The other ethnic groups, known as *"Côtiers"* (Coastal people), mostly of African and Arabic origins, live in the peripheral areas (or the *côte*). Although all of these different ethnic groups can communicate with each other using the common *Malagasy* language (classified as a Malayo-Polynesian language), the cultural divisions and rivalries continually threaten the political stability of the country. The most notable antagonism exists between *Merina* and *Côtiers*. The entente or discord between those two groups has strongly influenced the political and economic orientation of the whole country since independence (Archer, 1976). The population of Madagascar in 1980 was 8.8 million. It grew at an annual average growth rate of 2.8 per cent during the 1980s, and 2.9 per cent during the 1990s, and reached 15 million in 1999 (World Bank, 2001).

Numerous small political units (kingdoms or chiefdoms) evolved all over the island until the beginning of the 19th century, when the *Merina* kingdom unified two thirds of the country under a large political unit, known as the *Kingdom of Madagascar*. This kingdom established diplomatic relations with the major powers of the 19th century, including England, France, Germany and the United States, before it was defeated by France in 1896 (Deschamps, 1972). Subsequently, the island was colonized by France from 1896 to 1960.

At independence, Madagascar established a constitutional demo-cracy with a presidential system and one dominant party, the *Parti Social Democrate* (PSD). The first elected president, Philibert Tsira-nana, maintained strong economic, cultural, and military ties with

France. He also pursued moderate social welfare programs. In 1972, faced with a massive demonstration of students angered by the deterioration of the economy and the continued French domination, Philibert Tsiranana decided to step down. A military regime led by General Gabriel Ramanantsoa was established during a transitional period from 1972 to 1975. This military regime, marked by firm nationalism, initiated the so-called *Malgachisation*, which had as its goal giving a national character to the economy, the public administration, the national security and the education system. In connection with this new political orientation, the military regime withdrew Madagascar from the Franc monetary zone, displaced many French nationals from the public administration, and compelled the French military forces to evacuate their bases in Antananarivo and Antsiranana (formerly known as Diego Suarez). In addition, the French language was replaced by the Malagasy language as the educational language in primary and secondary schools (Covell, 1987; Archer, 1976).

In June 1975, following the resignation of General Gabriel Ramanantsoa and the subsequent assassination of his designated successor (Colonel Richard Ratsimandrava), Commander (later Admiral) Didier Ratsiraka took power and immediately established a socialist regime. Didier Ratsiraka's socialist regime officially lasted until 1992, when a massive democratic movement led to its abolition (Brown, 1997; Covell, 1987; Racine, 1983; Mukonoweshuro, 1994, 1990). In reality, however, the failure of his socialist development strategy forced Didier Ratsiraka to compromise his socialist orientation, and to agree with the IMF and the World Bank on the implementation of an SAP as early as 1982. This compelled him also to liberalize the economy and promote the private sector thereafter.

As a result of the democratic movement of 1991-1992, a new democratic constitution was written and adopted in 1992. This officially put an end to the socialist regime established by Didier Ratsiraka in 1975. Didier Ratsiraka had also to compete in a democratic presidential election in 1993, and lost to the leader of the opposition, Professor Albert Zafy. The 1992 democratic constitution set up a semi-presidential system, in which the President of the Republic was elected through universal suffrage, and the Prime Minister designated by the National Assembly. This system aggravated the political instability in the island during the period of 1993-1995. In order to solve this problem, President Zafy initiated a constitutional amendment in September 1995, which allowed him to appoint a Prime Minister of his own choice.   However, due to his inability to deal with the continued deterioration of the economy and his wrangling with the National Assembly, President Zafy was impeached in September 1996.   This gave Didier Ratsiraka the opportunity to come back in power after he won the presidential election held in 1997.   Ultimately, he lost the 2001 controversial presidential election to the businessman and Mayor of Antananarivo, Marc Ravalomanana (Versi, 2002; Misser, 2001; Brown, 1997).

The economy of Madagascar during the 1980s and 1990s was mainly based on the agricultural sector, which accounted for about 80 per cent of the country's export revenues, and about 40 per cent of its GDP, and engaged about 86 per cent of the labor force estimated to be 5.9 million in 1993 (IMF, 1997a; Tudor, 1997).   Rice is the main crop grown by more than 70 per cent of the population, and is also the staple food. Madagascar's cash crops are coffee and vanilla. In 1994, coffee accounted for about 24 per cent of the total export earnings and engaged 25 per cent of the working population. Madagascar was the world's largest exporter of vanilla until 1989, when it was pushed into the second place by Indonesia. Vanilla accounted for 17 per cent of Madagascar's total export revenue in 1994, but engaged less than 1 per cent of the working population. The United States and France are the main purchasers of Malagasy vanilla (Tudor, 1997).

During the 1980s, with assistance from Japan and France, shrimp fishing was developed, and in 1994 represented the third largest source of export revenue (after coffee and vanilla). Small quantities of lobster are also exported.   In addition, a tuna-canning complex has been established as a joint venture with a French company (Tudor, 1997).

The industrial sector accounted only for 13.8 per cent of Madagascar's GDP in 1994 and employed about 3 per cent of the working population. Food processing constituted half of all industrial value added. Textile was formerly the second largest sector but has been superseded by brewing, paper and soap (Tudor, 1997). There were also cement and fertilizer plants, but their production was limited. Since the introduction of a new investment code in 1986, which provided a package of incentives for domestic and foreign investors, an Export Processing Zone (EPZ) sector has been established,[2] and has attracted foreign investors, particularly from France, Italy, Mauritius and Hong Kong.

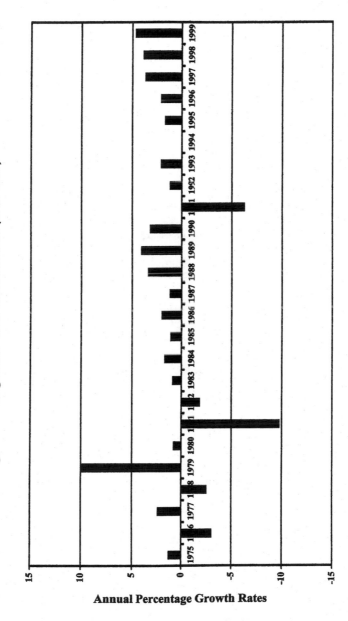

Fig. 6.1 - Madagascar: GDP Growth Rates (1975-1999)

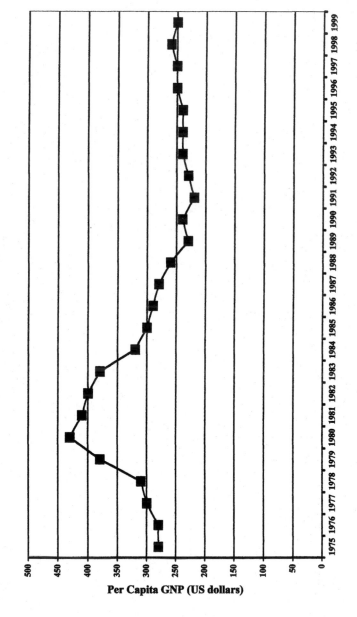

Fig. 6.2 - Madagascar: Per Capita GNP (1975-1999)

From 1999 onwards, as Anver Versi (2002) puts it, "a miracle of sorts seemed to have occurred" in Madagascar, as the economy grew by around 5 per cent in 1999 and 2000, and reached 6.7 per cent in 2001 (Versi 2002; IMF, 2001; World Bank 2001).[3] According to François Misser (2001), the main catalysts of this unprecedented economic growth were the sharp increase in FDI "from nothing to in the mid-1980s to $58.4 million in 1999," and the expansion of the EPZ sector. Indeed, the number of enterprises established in the EPZ sector increased from 267 enterprises employing about 35,000 workers in 1996 to 283 employing about 66,000 in 2000 (IMF, 2001).

Unfortunately, the dramatic political crisis of 2002, which followed the December 2001 presidential election, wiped out all the progress made since 1997, and brought the country's economic and social conditions back to their state in the 1980s (Versi, 2002). Indeed, according to a preliminary estimate of the World Bank and the IMF, this political crisis, which involved general strikes across the island, as well as armed conflicts between the partisans of the incumbent president, Didier Ratsiraka, and his challenger, Mark Ravalomanana, would have cost about $10 million a day to the economy of the country. And the EPZ sector, which was one of the main catalysts of the economic growth, was severely affected by this political crisis (Ranaivo, May 18, 2002). Thus, while Marc Ravalomanana was declared the winner of the 2001 presidential election, after an ultimate recount by the High Constitutional Court, he was presiding over a country devastated by prolonged general strikes and armed conflicts.

The Economic and Social Problems of Madagascar in the 1980s and UNPAAERD

Madagascar was facing a severe economic crisis at the end of the 1970s and the beginning of the 1980s. This crisis was characterized by the ups and downs of the GDP growth rates, and particularly by the loss of its creditworthiness within the international financial system (Tudor, 1997). In addition to these two phenomena, most of the characteristics of the critical economic and social conditions of Africa at the beginning of the 1980s were also present in Madagascar. These characteristics included:

- Falling per capita GNP,[4]
- Relatively high population growth rate,[5]

- Increasing external debt,[6] and
- Declining international assistance.[7]

The other specific aspects of the economic crisis in Madagascar during this period were related to the industrial sector and the transportation system.   According to Gilles Duruflé (1989), the industrial production declined by more than 25 per cent between 1980 and 1982, and the transportation system became dramatically deteriorated (due to lack of equipment, spare parts, and poor maintenance of infrastructure).   This exacerbated the internal disarticulation of the economy.

However, contrary to most African countries, the per capita food production did not dramatically decline in Madagascar, despite a slight decrease in agricultural production during the period of 1980-1985.[8] In addition, the degradation of the environment in the country was not as severe as in many countries on the continent, where it provoked widespread famine and hunger.

Many analysts agree that the major causes of the critical economic and social conditions of Madagascar at the beginning of the 1980s were the *particular political and economic history of the island*, and the *adoption of inappropriate development strategies and programs by successive Malagasy governments* (Tudor, 1997; Rajaonarivony, 1996; Duruflé, 1989).

Like many other African countries, Madagascar inherited from its former colonial power, France, a colonial trading economy, which was structured around the production and export of primary commodities (especially coffee and vanilla). Also like many other African countries, Madagascar implemented after independence an inward-looking development strategy based on import-substituting industrialization (ISI), pursued expensive social welfare programs, and sustained the growth of the public sector (Duruflé, 1989). In addition, the country had to deal with unfavorable geographic conditions that impeded internal and external transportation.[9] Moreover, the development of the island had been hampered by a long history and tradition of resistance of the rural societies to centralized power, and to modernization. Besides, the weakness of the market economy in the country limited its capacity to produce, export, import and invest (Duruflé, 1989).

Particularly, the nationalist and socialist development strategies adopted by the Malagasy governments between 1972 and 1982 constituted the direct causes of the critical economic and social conditions at the beginning of the 1980s. These strategies consisted in the nationalization of the economy and the implementation of the so-called program of *investissement à outrance* ("investment to the extreme limit") by the Malagasy government (Duruflé, 1989).

The nationalization of the economy was part of the *Malgachisation* initiated by the military regime under General Gabriel Ramanantsoa (1972-1975). It was a reaction against the domination by France of the economy, the public administration, the national security, and the education system of Madagascar since independence. In order to take control of these domains, the military government led by General Ramanantsoa decided to revise the cooperation accords with France, and initiate the processes of *Malgachisation* and nationalization of the economy. As a result, the military regime withdrew Madagascar from the Franc monetary zone, drove the French military forces out of the two military bases they maintained in the island (in Antananarivo and Antsiranana), and replaced many French nationals in the public administration with Malagasy nationals. The military government also began to nationalize some foreign companies controlling the production and distribution of basic necessities (such as rice, flour, sugar, petroleum, etc.) Didier Ratsiraka pursued the application of these measures of nationalization of the economy at the beginning of his socialist regime in 1975-1982. Particularly, he nationalized all banks and insurance companies, as well as most important companies managed by foreigners in the agricultural, industrial, and trade sectors (Mukonoweshuro, 1994 and 1991; Covell, 1987).

The immediate effects of these measures of *Malgachisation* and nationalization were disastrous. As Gilles Duruflé appropriately reports:

> Rather than unleashing new economic processes, the strategy of [Malgachisation and nationalization] quite rapidly provoked the tightening of constraints and a deterioration in the economic situation which was aggravated by the fluctuations of the international environment.
> The break with France, along with the measures taken to curtail foreign capital resulted in a drop in public and private capital inflows, and very probably as well, the *flight of capital*. The departure of a number of [French] expatriates, the disorganisation resulting from the implementation of certain measures to nationalise trade and commerce, led ultimately to a drop in exports, which was intensified by the deterioration in the terms of trade throughout the 1970s. (Duruflé, 1989: 176) (Emphasis Added)

The *flight of capital* mentioned by Gilles Duruflé in the above passage was confirmed by the data from the World Bank. Indeed, according to the World Bank, the FDI to Madagascar, which averaged $11 million a year at the beginning of the 1970s, turned into a flight of capital averaging $3 million a year during the period of 1977-1979 with a maximum of $6.6 millions in 1979. Since then, the flow of FDI to the country completely stopped until 1989, seven years after the first agreement with the Bretton Woods institutions on the implementation of SAP.

In addition to the measures of *Malagachisation* and nationalization, Didier Ratsiraka decided also to undertake a massive investment program during the period of 1978-1980. This program, known as *investissement à outrance* ("investment to the extreme limit"), was based on borrowing and financial assistance from socialist countries, particularly the Soviet Union. The ultimate goal of this program was to achieve autonomous development, self-sufficiency and self-reliance in food and industrial production within a "society of equality and justice" (Ratsiraka, 1975). During this period of *investissement à outrance*, the gross domestic investment rose from an annual average of 8.1 per cent of the GDP in 1975-1977 to 16.1 per cent in 1979, and 15 per cent in 1980. At the same time, the total external debt jumped, in current prices, from an annual average of $292 million in 1977 to $778.6 million in 1979, and $1,223 million in 1980.

However, as Gilles Duruflé (1989) points out, this program of *investment à outrance* was undertaken in the "most unfavorable conditions," and the economic and financial consequences were disastrous. In connection with this, Gilles Duruflé reports that the investments were "badly conceived and uncontrolled [and] did not contribute to unblocking the bottlenecks of the Malgache economy (transportation, weak integration, disarticulation). On the contrary because of the rationing of which they were the immediate cause, they contributed to intensifying these bottlenecks" (Duruflé, 1989: 177).

Furthermore, he notes that:

> From a financial standpoint, [these investments] were the cause of an extremely onerous debt burden (private borrowing, loans, suppliers' credits) contracted at a very importune moment, that of the downturn in prices for agricultural primary resources, the second oil shock, the rise in the dollar and in interest rates, together with the withdrawal from the Franc zone which deprived Madagascar of an important means of

absorbing the crisis. (Duruflé, 1989: 177)

The combined effects of the measures of *Malgachisation*, nationalization, and *investissement à outrance* provoked a total disruption of the Malagasy economy during the period of 1980-1982. As shown in Figure 6.1, the growth rates of the GDP were typically erratic during the period of 1975-1981. They jumped to a one-time high of 9.9 per cent in 1979, and then dropped to its lowest level of 9.8 per cent in 1981.[10] Particularly, by this time, Madagascar lost its creditworthiness within the international financial market as many of its traditional creditors and suppliers refused to grant credit to its government (Tudor, 1997). It was this loss of creditworthiness that compelled Didier Ratsiraka's socialist regime to reach an agreement with the IMF, the "lender of last resort," and the World Bank in 1982 (Brown, 1997; Tudor, 1997; Rajaonarivony, 1996). This was the only way for the Malagasy government to recover its creditworthiness, and, most importantly, to obtain more ODA and debt arrangements from the international donors, as well as to attract more FDI.

The SAP implemented in Madagascar during the 1980s mainly consisted of three sets of measures: (1) measures related to the *macroeconomic stabilization*, (2) measures related to *price liberalization*, and (3) measures related to the *promotion of open market economy and private sector* (Tudor, 1997; Duruflé, 1989).[11]

1. The measures related to the *macroeconomic stabilization* included:
    *   Restriction of money and credit;
    *   Devaluation and tying of the Malagasy franc to a basket of foreign currencies;
    *   Institutionalization of a flexible rate of exchange, subject to revision every trimester and devaluations in relation to the basket of currencies;
    *   Reduction of the deficit in public finances, which included reduction in the investment budget and a ceiling of salary increases.

2. The measures related to *price liberalization* included:
    *   Abolition of subsidies for consumer goods, such as rice;
    *   Increases in agricultural prices;
    *   Progressive liberalization of industrial prices;

- Progressive liberalization of exchange controls and of the system of currency allocation.

3. The measures related to the *promotion of open market economy and private sector* were contained in a new code of investment which provided incentives for domestic as well as foreign investors.

In exchange for the implementation of these measures, Madagascar received from the IMF a stand-by loan of $80 million in 1982, and another stand-by arrangement of SDR 29.5 million in 1985. In addition, the World Bank provided credit assistance to industry (CASI) valued at $40 million in 1985, and another $60 million for credit assistance to agriculture (CASA) in 1986. Besides, many capitalist developed countries, particularly France, Germany, and the United States, contributed to the solution of the economic crisis through increased ODA and debt arrangement (Duruflé, 1989).

The 1982 agreement with the Bretton Woods institutions solved the problem of creditworthiness by giving back to Madagascar the ability to borrow not only from these institutions, but also from the capitalist developed countries. At the same time, this agreement gave the country the opportunity to get more ODA and debt arrangements from the capitalist developed countries and, most importantly, to attract more FDI.[12] This agreement also allowed Madagascar to correct the mistakes of the 1970s, especially the adoption of the measures of *Malgachisation*, nationalization and *investissement à outrance*.

The case of Madagascar clearly demonstrates the alliance between the Bretton Woods institutions, the capitalist developed countries, and the MNCs. Indeed, it reveals that the flows of ODA and FDI from the capitalist developed countries depended on the agreement between this country and the Bretton Woods institutions on the implementation of an SAP.

However, despite the increase of ODA and FDI, and despite the debt arrangements with the international donors, the social and political costs of the SAP were relatively high for the Malagasy people and political leaders. As Gill Tudor (1997) points out, the increase in payments to farmers and the liberalization of the rice trade in 1983-1984 generated a significant rise in the cost of living. At the same time, the successive devaluation of the Malagasy Franc, combined with the inability of the government to increase the wages of nonagricultural workers, "placed the cost of basic necessities beyond the means of the average Malagasy" (Tudor, 1997: 572). As a result, the second half of the 1980s was marked by periodic riots, which culminated in 1991 in a general strike demanding the abolition of the socialist regime and the establishment of democracy (Brown, 1997; Mukonoweshuro, 1994 and 1990).

In evaluating the consequences of the SAP implemented in Madagascar during the 1980s, most analysts concluded that the overall results of this program were mixed (Tudor, 1997; Rajaonarivony, 1996; Dorosh and Bernier, 1994; Duruflé, 1989; Ramahatra, 1989). In addition to the social and political costs mentioned earlier, Gill Tudor (1997) emphasizes the dramatic increase of the total external debt of Madagascar, which reached $3.6 billion in 1988, and $3.9 billion in 1990. According to the author (1997), despite the "overall improvements of Madagascar's economic conditions," the island was not only increasingly indebted, but also increasingly dependent on foreign aid. Narisoa Rajaonarivony (1996) also argues that while the SAP particularly contributed to an improvement in Madagascar's balance of payments, it was unsuccessful in controlling inflation and reducing the external debt of the country.

Nevertheless, despite these negative impacts, we have to recognize that the most important achievement of this SAP was to reestablish the creditworthiness of Madagascar. In this sense, it can be argued that the economic and social conditions in the country could have been worse had the Malagasy government failed to reach an agreement with the Bretton Woods institutions in 1982 and started to implement the SAP thereafter. Moreover, thanks to the SAP, the Malagasy government had also the opportunity to correct the mistakes it made during the 1970s. As a result, the confidence of the foreign investors was recovered by the end of the 1980s, as a number of foreign banks and companies began to operate in the country (Tudor, 1997). As a matter of fact, the flows of FDI to Madagascar resumed in 1989, seven years after the adoption of the SAP by the Malagasy government, and three years after the publication of a new investment code in 1986, which provided incentives for domestic as well as foreign investors. Furthermore, Figure 6.1 clearly demonstrates that the growth rates of the GDP have been constantly positive between 1983 and 1990.[13]

Madagascar was already implementing its SAP with the Bretton Woods institutions when the UN General Assembly adopted UNPAAERD in 1986. Like many other African countries, Madagascar did not oppose the adoption of UNPAAERD, nor did it try to implement this UN development program. Thus, in order to understand the potential failure of UNPAAERD with respect to Madagascar, we need to discuss whether this program could have been used to solve the economic and social problems of this country in the 1980s.

As mentioned earlier, the agreement with the Bretton Woods institutions allowed Madagascar to address the urgent problem of creditworthiness, which prevented the country from continuing to do business on the world market. In addition, the implementation of the SAP also allowed the country to correct the adoption of inappropriate development strategies and programs, which were at the origins of the total disruption of the economy at the beginning of the 1980s. Furthermore, the agreement with the Bretton Woods institutions and the implementation of the SAP made the country to be more attractive to ODA and FDI.

On these issues and others, UNPAAERD appeared to be totally useless. First, with regard to the loss of creditworthiness, there was no measure in this UN development program that could address this problem. In fact, only an agreement with the IMF, the "lender of the last resort," could solve this problem. As mentioned earlier, the most important role of the IMF was to provide loans to countries experiencing balance of payments problems, which would allow them to recover their creditworthiness. However, while the IMF did not endorse UNPAAERD, the UN, expected by the African countries to replace this institution, could not play this role. Therefore, an African country like Madagascar that wanted to recover its creditworthiness in the international financial market had no other choice than to agree with the IMF and the World Bank and, at the same time, to abandon the implementation of UNPAAERD, which could not be used to address this pressing problem.

Second, the development strategies and programs adopted by Madagascar between 1972 and 1982 were based on the same type of inward-looking development strategy as UNPAAERD, which was focused on the development of agriculture and other sectors in support of agriculture, in order to achieve food self-reliance and self-sufficiency. While the means might have been different, the objective of self-reliance and self-sufficiency contained in UNPAAERD was very similar to that of the measures of *Malgachisation*, nationalization, and *investissement à outrance* adopted by Madagascar between 1972 and 1982. As discussed earlier, however, the adoption of these measures led to the total disruption of the Malagasy economy at the beginning of the 1980s. Therefore, the implementation of UN-PAAERD in the 1980s would have led to the same mistakes, and would have even worsened the economic and social problems of the country.

Finally, although the implementation of UNPAAERD would require an increase in ODA to Africa, this program actually failed to attract the international donors and investors. As a matter of fact, it was not endorsed neither by the capitalist developed countries nor the Bretton Woods institutions, which both continued to advocate the SAPs and conditioned their financial support to African countries on the implementation of these programs. Moreover, UNPAAERD did not offer any incentive such as tax holydays and preferential treatments that would attract domestic and foreign investors. Therefore, if Madagascar tried to implement UNPAAERD instead of its SAP, it would not have recovered its creditworthiness, nor would it have attracted more ODA and FDI in the 1980s.

In sum, UNPAAERD clearly appeared to be useless for Madagascar in the 1980s, which was struggling to recover its creditworthiness, correct its past mistakes of adopting inappropriate development strategies and programs, and attract more ODA and FDI. As we will see, the second UN development program, UNNADAF, could not fare better than UNPAAERD.

The Economic and Social Problems of Madagascar in the 1990s and UNNADAF

Madagascar enjoyed relatively high and constant GDP growth rates, averaging 3.5 per cent a year, during the period of 1988-1990. However, the GDP growth rates suddenly dropped to -6.7 per cent in 1991, and remained at a very low level, averaging 0.0 per cent a year, from 1991 to 1996.[14] In addition to these declining GDP growth rates, the economic and social conditions of the country at the end of the 1980s and at the beginning of the 1990s, were also characterized by:

- Declining per capita GNP,[15]
- Increasing population growth rate,[16] and
- Increasing external debt.[17]

In explaining the deterioration of the Malagasy economy at the beginning of the 1990s, many analysts point to the following factors:

1. The persistence of the political instability in the island since 1991, and
2. The reluctance of most political leaders to pursue the implementation of the SAP with the Bretton Woods institutions.

1. The persistence of the political instability in the island since 1991: There were two main sources of political instability in Madagascar at the beginning of the 1990s, both of which affected the economic performance of the country:

- The transition from the socialist regime to a new democratic regime, and
- The semi-presidential system introduced by the democratic constitution adopted in 1992.

The political transition in 1991-1992 was a long and painful process. It took Didier Ratsiraka about seven months of general strikes across the island (from May to December 1991), marked by violent confrontations between the opposition and the police forces, before he decided to abolish the socialist regime, adopt a new democratic constitution, and organize a democratic presidential and legislative elections (Brown, 1997;   Mukonoweshuro, 1994).   Following the general strikes, it also took the country a long period of 18 months to draft and adopt a new democratic constitution, and to hold the democratic elections. As a result, it was only in June 1993 (two year after the beginning of the democratic movement) that Madagascar had officially a new democratic regime with a new President, Albert Zafy, and a new governmental coalition led by Prime Minister Francisque Ravony. During these two years of intense political activities (May 1991 to June 1993), many political and economic arrangements established by the socialist regime, including the agreements with the Bretton Woods institutions, were suspended.[18] In addition, because of these intense political activities, the economic activities in general slowed down across the island.

The new democratic constitution established a semi-presidential system in which the President of the Republic – Chief of the State – was elected through universal suffrage, and the Prime Minister – Chief of the Government – was designated by the majority at the National Assembly.[19] This system created an executive branch with two competing (if not conflicting) heads. These two heads were theoretically provided with equal power, and no one had power to influence or dismiss the other. From the beginning, this semi-presidential system was complicated by the fact that neither President Albert Zafy nor Prime Minister Francisque Ravony commanded a stable majority at the National Assembly, and the fact that the National Assembly itself was composed by members from 25 different political parties, which formed shifting coalitions depending on the issues debated (Brown, 1997). As a result, the new political system was highly unstable and unpredictable. As an illustration of this instability and unpredictability, in 1994, Prime Minister Ravony reached an agreement on a new SAP with the Bretton Woods institutions, and his government began to implement some of the measures included in this program. However, with a strong support from the National Assembly, President Albert Zafy was able to stop the full implementation of this program (Brown, 1997; IMF, 1997).

2. *The reluctance of most political leaders to pursue the implementation of the SAP:* In the 1990s, the Malagasy political leaders opposing the SAP included the former President Albert Zafy, and the former Speaker of the National Assembly Rev. Richard Andriamanjato. The conditions imposed by the Bretton Woods institutions and the international donors in the 1990s were harsh and directly hurt the constituents of these powerful political leaders. Indeed, by this time, the Bretton Woods institutions conditions included "the floating of the Malagasy franc (which resulted in an immediate devaluation), the removal of price controls, further privatization, and measures to reduce budgetary expenditure" (Tudor, 1997: 569). However, in the absence of any viable alternative economic policy, stopping the implementation of the SAP meant also stopping the financial support from the Bretton Woods institutions and the capitalist developed countries.

The Malagasy political leaders were not able to design and implement any viable alternative to the SAPs. None of the solutions they tried at the beginning of the 1990s worked. One of these solutions was the so-called *financement parallèle* ("parallel financing"), which was designed to bypass the Bretton Woods institutions by "placing large amounts of promissory notes on concessional terms in the international market" (IMF, 1997: 13). The whole scheme failed miserably, because there was only one private investor involved: Prince Constantin of Liechtenstein, whose company, Flamco, had a subsidiary established in Madagascar. In addition, in October 1994, Flamco's directors, including two of the Speaker's sons, "were accused of misappropriating funds advanced by the government and other irregularities" (Brown, 1997: 568).

In order to deal with the political instability and the reluctance of the political leadership to pursue the SAP, a constitutional amendment and a formal agreement with the Bretton Woods institutions were necessary. In connection with this, the National Assembly passed a constitutional amendment in September 1995 which allowed the President of the Republic to appoint and dismiss the Prime Minister. This constitutional amendment greatly strengthened the power of the President. At the same time, it unified the executive branch, and made it more accountable to the National Assembly.

Provided with his new power, President Albert Zafy appointed Emmanuel Rakotovahiny as a new Prime Minister. However, for different reasons including his inability to solve the country's serious economic and social problems, the government led by Prime Minister Emmanuel Rakotovahiny was censured by the National Assembly in May 1996. Consequently, President Albert Zafy had to appoint Norbert Ratsirahonana as a new Prime Minister.

Nevertheless, the political fights between President Zafy and the majority at the National Assembly (the so-called "G7 group") continued well beyond the appointment of Prime Minister Ratsirahonana. Ultimately, the majority at the National Assembly decided to impeach President Zafy in September 1996. An anticipated presidential election was held in 1996-1997, which resulted in the victory of the former President Didier Ratsiraka. Following this presidential election, a legislative election held in 1997 also resulted in a clear victory of Didier Ratsiraka's political party (AREMA), which won a majority at the National Assembly. Consequently, some analysts argued that the return of Didier Ratsiraka to power and the victory of his political party finally contributed to the political stabilization of the country since 1997 (Versi, 2002; Missier, 2001).

With regard to the reluctance of the political leaders to pursue the implementation the SAP, the French government made it clear in 1994 that it would suspend all assistance to Madagascar unless its government reached an agreement with the Bretton Woods institutions (Brown, 1997). Consequently, once in office, the new Prime Minister, Norbert Ratsirahonana, appointed by President Albert Zafy in May 1996, quickly reached an agreement with the representatives of the

Bretton Woods institutions on a new SAP. He also took advantage of the political situation to have the National Assembly approve it.

The new SAP was contained in what was known as the *Document Cadre de Politique Economique* (Economic Policy Framework Document) (*DCPE*) (Tudor, 1997; Brown, 1997). In this document, the Malagasy government formally announced its commitment to establish "a free market economy, characterized by an economic and social environment favorable to the development of the private sector, the attraction of foreign investment, the disengagement of the state from the sector of production, and an efficient method of fighting poverty" (Republique de Madagascar, 1996: 1) (Own translation). The main objective of this new program was to achieve an annual average growth rate of GDP higher than 4 per cent by the year 1999.

The *DCPE* contained four sets of measures related to the following domains:

1. Measures related to the *macroeconomic and financial policy*, which included:
    *   Reduction of inflation from 4.9 per cent in 1996 to 3 per cent by 1999;
    *   Transformation of the budget deficit of 1.1 per cent of the GDP in 1996 to an excess of 0.7 per cent by 1999;
    *   Reduction of the balance of payments deficit from 7 per cent of the GDP in 1996 to 5 per cent by 1999; and
    *   Maintenance of an adequate interest rate by the Central Bank, and tight money control.

2. Measures related to the *functions of the state*, which included:
    *   Disengagement of the state from the economic activities;
    *   focus of the state on the creation and protection of the economic and social environment conducive to economic activities;
    *   Reform of the public administration in order to ensure competence and integrity; and
    *   Decentralization of power and decision making.

3. The measures related to *promotion of the private sector*, which included:
    *   Creation of a secure environment for domestic and foreign investors;

- Liberalization of price and exchange;
- Access of the foreign investors to land property;
- Abolition of the state monopoly in the domain of energy, telecommunication, and air transportation;
- Privatization of the major public enterprises, including the national petroleum company (SOLIMA), the national airline company (Air Madagascar), and two national commercial banks (BFV and BTM); and
- Establishment of tax incentives for exporters and foreign investors.

4. Measures related to the so-called *sectorial policies*, which included:
- Poverty eradication by providing primary education, basic health and public security to everyone;
- Protection of the environment by applying the National Charter of Environment; and
- Maintenance and development of adequate infrastructures.

Upon his return to power in 1997, Didier Ratsiraka and the government led by Prime Minister Tantely Andrianarivo continued the implementation this new SAP. As a result, by the end of the 1990s, the positive effects of this program were acclaimed by many observers, some of which equated the economic success of Madagascar at the end of the 1990s to a "miracle" (Versi, 2002; Misser, 2001).

The most important effect of the implementation of this new SAP was above all the resumption of the financial support from the Bretton Woods institutions and the capitalist developed countries. In connection with this, in November 1996, Madagascar received from the World Bank the first portion of the enhanced structural adjustment facility (ESAF), which was worth $118 million. The disbursement of the second portion of $60 million was conditional on the progress made by the Malagasy government, particularly in the privatization of the national petroleum company (SOLIMA), the national airline company (Air Madagascar), and the two remaining national commercial banks (BFV and BTM) (Tudor, 1997). Moreover, the confidence of the foreign investors was recovered, as the FDI reached $16 million in 1998 and $58 million in 1999, compared to an average of $10 million annually during the period of 1994-1997. As a result, the GDP growth rates reached 3.9 per cent in 1998, 4.7 per cent in 1999, and 6.7 in 2000.[20]

When UNNADAF was adopted by the UN General Assembly in 1991, Madagascar was in the midst of political turmoil, and its political leaders were so busy with their intense political activities that they had no time at all to deal with the economic and social problems of the country. However, when the new government led by Prime Minister Francisque Ravony was established in June 1993, they were divided into two groups: the first group, represented by President Albert Zafy, was in favor of the so-called *financement parallèle* ("parallel financing") in conjunction with − if not, outside of − the traditional financial flows from the Bretton Woods institutions and the capitalist developed countries; and the second group, represented by Prime Minister Francisque Ravony, was in favor of the continuation of the SAP with the Bretton Woods institutions. The first group dominated until September 1996, when the National Assembly adopted the *Document Cadre de Politique Economique* (Economic Policy Framework Document) (*DCPE*), which contained the new SAP. These events clearly show that UNNADAF was not considered as a viable alternative by the Malagasy political leaders. However, in order to understand the failure of UNNADAF with respect to Madagascar, we need to discuss whether this UN development program could have been used to solve the economic and social problems of this country in the 1990s.

The two major factors that caused the poor economic performance of Madagascar at the beginning of the 1990s were the persistence of the political instability and the reluctance of most political leaders to pursue the implementation of the SAP with the Bretton Woods institutions. If we refer to the measures contained in UNNADAF,[21] we have to recognize that this UN development program could not be used neither to ensure political stability nor to serve as a viable alternative to the SAP in the case of Madagascar.

First, on the issue of political instability, UNNADAF could not be blamed for not containing specific measures to ensure political stability in an individual African country like Madagascar, where constitutional amendment and democratic elections were necessary for this purpose. However, it can be argued that this UN development program was flawed, because it was based on a sweeping generalization about all African countries, and did not recognize the fact that political instability constituted one of the most important causes of the disastrous economic and social conditions in Africa in the 1980s and 1990s. In fact, these African countries did not have the same political, economic and social conditions that would justify the design of a single development program applicable to all of them. Consequently, each African country should have had its own development program, and in the case of Madagascar the existence of political stability should have constituted a prerequisite of any development program.

Second, it is true that UNNADAF contained some measures on the continuation of "necessary reforms" and "improvement of domestic economic management, including effective mobilization and utilization of domestic resources,"[22] which were parts of the SAPs sponsored by the Bretton Woods institutions. However, there was no real intention to implement these measures on the part of most African countries. They were included in UNNADAF just to accommodate the Bretton Woods institutions and the capitalist developed countries in the hope that these international donors would support this UN development program (Mongula, 1994). As a matter of fact, the most important measures put forward by UNNADAF concerned, on the one hand the implementation of the measures for import-substituting industrialization (ISI) prescribed by the *African Alternative Framework to Structural Adjustment Programmes for Socio-Economic Recovery and Transformation (AAF-SAP)*,[23] and on the other hand "the promotion of regional and subregional economic cooperation and integration," including the "establishment of the African Economic Community."[24]

The measures for import-substituting industrialization (ISI) contained in UNNADAF were based on the same type of inward-looking development strategy as the measures of *Malgachisation*, nationa-lization and *investissement à outrance* adopted by Madagascar between 1972 and 1982, and which were the causes of the total disruption of the economy at the beginning of the 1980s. Therefore, in the case of this country, the implementation of UNNADAF in the 1990s would have led to the same mistakes, and would have worsened its economic and social problems. Furthermore, like UNPAAERD in the 1980s, UNNADAF was not supported neither by the Bretton Woods institutions nor by the capitalist developed countries. Consequently, it was not likely to attract more ODA and FDI to Madagascar, as the SAP sponsored by the Bretton Woods institutions did in the 1980s and 1990s.

With regard to the promotion of regional and subregional economic cooperation and integration, hundreds of African organizations of economic cooperation and integration have been created since the 1960s, but none of them has been as successful as the European Union (or the former European Community). The major cause of their failure had to do with the weaknesses and similarities of the African economies. These economies generally produced similar agricultural and mineral products, which drove them to compete against each other instead of becoming complementary. Therefore, in the case of Madagascar, there was no guarantee that the promotion of regional and subregional economic cooperation and integration would have compensated the loss of ODA and FDI endured by this country if it was to abandon the implementation of the SAP with the Bretton Woods institutions.

In sum, like UNPAAERD, UNNADAF was clearly useless in the case of Madagascar, which was coping with political instability and struggling to attract more ODA and FDI in the 1990s. This case also demonstrates that in order to be useful and efficient, a development program must be country-specific. That is, it must deal with the specific political, economic and social problems of the country for which it was designed.

Conclusion

The case of Madagascar clearly demonstrates that UNPAAERD and UNNADAF were not very useful in dealing with the particular political, economic and social problems of this country in the 1980s and 1990s. These UN development programs were based on the same type of inward-looking development strategy as the measures of *Malgachisation*, nationalization, and *investissement à outrance* adopted in Madagascar during the 1970s, which were the causes of the total disruption of its economy at the beginning of the 1980s. Therefore unless the Malagasy political leaders were completely out of touch with the reality, they would not repeat the same mistakes in the 1980s and 1990s by implementing these UN development programs.

However, on two occasions, the Bretton Woods institutions saved the Malagasy economy from bankruptcy: first by providing assistance in the recovery of its creditworthiness at the beginning of the 1980s, and second by helping to attract more ODA and FDI in the 1990s. The case of Mauritius, one the most successful economies in Africa, will further demonstrate the usefulness of the Bretton Woods institutions and the total failure of the two UN development programs.

Notes

[1] The term *Malagasy* (or *Malgache*, in French language) is used to describe the people of Madagascar and their language.

[2] As in the case of Mauritius (See Chapter 7) and most South East Asian countries, the EPZ sector in Madagascar was established in order to attract domestic and foreign investment, by providing different kinds of incentives, including tax holidays, cheap labor, etc.

[3] See Fig. 6.1 – Madagascar: GDP Growth Rates (1975-1999), above, p. 105.

[4] According to the World Bank, the per capita GNP for Madagascar fell from $430 in 1980 to $300 in 1985; that is a decline of 6.3 per cent a year, compared to a decline of 3.1 per cent for the whole African continent (World Bank, 2001). See Fig. 6.1 – Madagascar: GDP Growth Rates (1975-1999), above, p. 105, and Fig. 6.2 – Madagascar: Per Capita GNP (1975-1999), above, p. 106.

[5] According to the World Bank, the annual average percentage growth of the population in Madagascar during the 1980s was 2.8 (World Bank, 2001: 6).

[6] According to the World Bank, the total external debt of Madagascar increased, in current prices, from $1.2 billion in 1980 to $2.7 billion in 1985, which represented 112 per cent of the real GDP (World Bank, 2001).

[7] According to the World Bank and the Organisation for Economic Co-operation and Development (OECD), the net ODA to Madagascar decreased, in current prices, from an average of $231 million during the period of 1979-1982 to an average of $173 million during the period of 1983-1985, before it jumped to $310 million in 1986 and $332 million in 1987 (World Bank, 2001; OECD, various years).

[8] According the World Bank, while the index of per capita food production in Madagascar increased from 83 in 1980 to 93 in 1986, the index of agricultural production fell respectively from 116 to 108 (World Bank, 1997a: 222- 225).

[9] Gilles Duruflé explains how the geography of the island impeded transportation as follows: "This is the case of internal transportation (the island is vast and mountainous). It is the case as well for external transportation. Madagascar is not close to any major markets, and given its weak economic power, it has always been the victim of unfavorable shipping costs" (Duruflé, 1989: 172).

[10] See Fig. 6.1 – Madagascar: GDP Growth Rates (1975-1999), above, p. 105.

[11] The third component of the SAPs related to the role of the state, mentioned by Lionel Demery (1994) was not included in this program.

[12] During the period of 1982-1990, while the ODA from the socialist countries declined from $82 million to zero, the ODA from the capitalist developed countries increased from $159 million to $311 millions (OECD, various years).

[13] Ses Fig. 6.1 – Madagascar: GDP Growth Rates (1975-1999), above, p. 105.

[14] See Fig. 6.2 – Madagascar: Per Capita GNP (1975-1999), above, p. 106.

[15] The per capita GNP fell from an average of $240 during the period of 1988-1990 to an average of $230 during the period of 1990- 1996. See Fig. 6.1 – Madagascar: Per Capita GNP (1975-1999), above, p. 106.

[16] The annual average growth rate of the population in Madagascar was 2.8 per cent during the 1980s. This rate increased to 2.9 per cent during the 1990s compared to 2.5 per cent for the whole African continent (World Bank, 2001:6).

[17] According to the World Bank, the total external debt of Madagascar increased, in current prices, from $3.7 billion in 1990 to $4.3 billion in 1995, which represented 153 per cent of the real GDP in 1996 (compared to 113 per cent in 1985) (World Bank, 2001: 174).

[18] As Gill Tudor (1997) points out, an important public investment program for the period of 1991-1993, valued at $1 billion, financed by the World Bank and other international donors, was initiated in 1991. This program was suspended, because of the general strikes in 1991 and the subsequent political instability prevailing in the country.

[19] The roles and functions of the President of the Republic and the Prime Minister were defined by the constitution. Basically, the President was responsible for the national defense and the foreign affairs of the country (Malagasy Constitution of August 19, 1992, Art. 55 and 56), and the Prime Minister was responsible for all domestic affairs (Malagasy Constitution of August 19, 1992, Art. 61- 65). But there were some areas in which their respective roles and functions overlapped, and created confusion and conflict. That was, for instance, the case of the relations of Madagascar with the Bretton Woods institutions.

[20] See Fig. 6.1 – Madagascar: GDP Growth Rates (1975-1999), above, p. 105.

[21] UN document No. A/RES/46/151 of 18 December 1991, annex II.B. See Chapter 3, above.

[22] UN document No. A/RES/46/151 of 18 December 1991, annex II.B.1(a), parag.10.

[23] UN document No. A/RES/46/151 of 18 December 1991, annex II.B.1(a), parag.10.

[24] UN document No. A/RES/46/151 of 18 December 1991, annex II.B.1(a), parag.11.

Chapter 7

The Case of Mauritius

At independence on March 12, 1968, Mauritius was said to be "the paradigm of a small isolated, poor, dependent country," or "the Third World's Third World" (Houbert, 1981: 75). However, by the end of the 1980s, the economic and social development of this country was widely acclaimed as a "success story" (Bowman, 1991), or even an "economic miracle" in Sub-Saharan Africa (Kibazo, January 1996; Dutoil, 1993, October 23). Indeed, during the 1980s and 1990s, the GDP growth rates of Mauritius averaged 5.4 per cent a year, and its per capita GNP jumped from $1240 in 1980 to $3800 in 1997 (Subramanian and Roy, 2001; World Bank, 2001, 1997a, 1995).[1] The case of Mauritius, along with a very few other countries like Botswana, demonstrate that economic and social development is possible in Africa.

This chapter discusses the case of Mauritius within the context of UNPAAERD and UNNADAF. In doing so, it presents a general background about Mauritius. Next, referring to each UN development program, it discusses the economic and social problems faced by Mauritius along with the solutions adopted by its government, and demonstrates how and why each one of these UN development programs failed to solve these problems.

General Background About Mauritius

One of the smallest countries in the world, the Republic of Mauritius comprises the main island Mauritius and other smaller surrounding islands (including Rodrigues, the Agalega Islands and the Cargados Carajos Shoals). Mauritius lies in the Indian Ocean about 500 miles (800 kilometers) east of Madagascar, and covers an area of

720 square miles (2,040 square kilometers) ("Mauritius: Physical and Social Geography," 1997).

Mauritius was discovered by the Portuguese at the beginning of the 16th century. However, it was, the Dutch who first attempted to occupy the island between 1638 and 1710. After the Dutch, the French acquired the island in 1715. They imported slaves from Madagascar and the East coast of Africa in order to develop their sugar cane plantations. However, as a result of the Napoleonic wars in Europe, the British took control of the island in 1810. They freed the African slaves and imported indentured laborers from India and China in order to maintain the production of sugar cane. As a result of this British immigration policy, the population of Indian origin became the majority of the Mauritian population by the end of the 19th century (Bowman, 1991).

The population of Mauritius in 1980 was 0.97 million. It increased by an annual average of 0.9 per cent during the 1980s and by 1.3 per cent during the 1990s, and reached 1.17 million in 1999 (World Bank, 2001: 6). Emigration and low birth rates explain these exceptionally slow growth rates of the population (Bowman, 1991).

At independence, Mauritius inherited a democratic parliamentary regime from the British, and it is now recognized as one of the few stable democracies in Africa. The first Prime Minister, Seewoosagur Ramgoolam, a leader of the Mauritian Labour Party (MLP), pursued different programs of public-sector investment and social welfare (IMF, 1997; Meisenhelder, 1997; Bowman, 1991). He initiated in the early 1970s the *Travail pour Tous* ("Work for All") program, which consisted of creating low-paid jobs throughout the public sector. This program was described by some analysts as a "form of redistribution of income, rather than a productive form of labor" (Bowman, 1991: 116). It was also during the Ramgoolam era that Mauritius implemented its SAP with the Bretton Woods institutions, along with the creation and expansion of its Export Processing Zone (EPZ) sector, the development of tourism, and the modernization of the sugar industry, which were the engines of the Mauritian economy. Despite the opposition from the left-wing political parties, particularly the "Mouvement Militant Mauricien" (MMM), and from the business community, particularly the so-called "sugar barons," Ramgoolam stayed in power until June 1982, when the alliance of the MMM and the "Parti Socialiste Mauricien" (PSM) won all of the seats at the Legislative Assembly ("Mauritius: Recent History," 1997; Bowman, 1991).

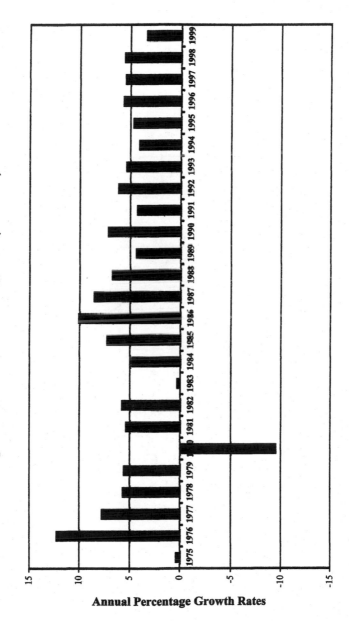

Fig. 7.1 - Mauritius: GDP Growth Rates (1975-1999)

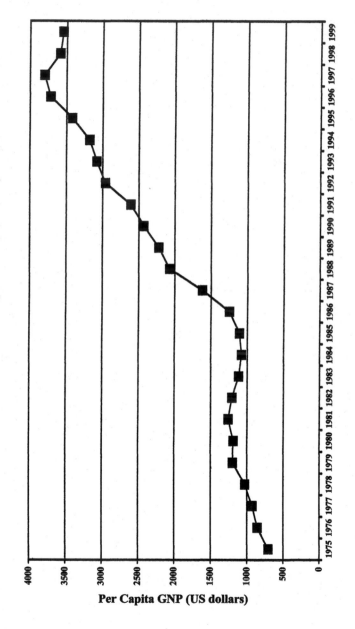

Fig. 7.2 - Mauritius: Per capita GNP (1975-1999)

As a result of the 1982 sweeping victory of the MMM-PSM coalition, Anerood Jugnauth, a leader of the MMM, became Prime Minister. Subsequently, from 1982 to 1995, despite a series of political scandals and the opposition from rival political parties, Anerood Jugnauth and his new political party, "Mouvement Socialiste Mauricien" (MSM) dominated the Mauritian politics and government ("Mauritius: Recent History," 1997; Bowman, 1991). The Jugnauth era ended with the December 1995 general election, during which the MLP-MMM coalition won the majority of seats at the Legislative Assembly. As a result of this general election, Navin Ramgoolam (son of Seewoosagur Ramgoolam), the new leader of the MLP, became Prime Minister.

With regard to the economic domain, it was during the Jugnauth era (1982-1995) that Mauritius achieved its "economic miracle" and moved from the status of agricultural country to that of a "Newly Industrialized Country" (NIC) (Kearney, 1990). Before this era, the Mauritian economy was dominated by sugar production, and its growth highly dependent on the climatic conditions and changes in the international price of sugar. Since the Jugnauth era, the dominance of the sugar industry was progressively counterbalanced by manufacturing in the EPZ sector, and tourism (Sparks, 1997; Bowman, 1990).

During the 1980s and 1990s, sugar production occupied a total of 84,400 ha (almost one-half of the entire surface area of the island and 87 per cent of arable land), and engaged some 70,000 workers (15 per cent of the labor force in 1987) during the crop season between July and December, and 60,000 during the inter-crop season (Sparks, 1997). During some exceptional years (for example in 1986), sugar production reached 700,000 tons, but the annual average production was about 600,000 tons. At the beginning of the 1980s, sugar production accounted for about 13 per cent of the GDP and 23 per cent of the total export earnings. However, by 1994, it only accounted for 9 per cent of the GDP and 15 per cent of the total export earnings (Sparks, 1997). Until 1975, most of the Mauritian sugar was sold to Great Britain at a guaranteed price, under the Commonwealth Sugar Agreement. This arrangement was then replaced by the Sugar Protocol of the Lomé Conventions, signed between the European Community (EC), which is now known as the European Union (EU), and the group of African, Caribbean, and Pacific (ACP) countries, which included Mauritius. Under the Lomé Conventions, Mauritius received an annual quota of 585,000 tons of raw sugar, and was the principal exporter of sugar to

European countries. Other important customers for the Mauritian sugar were the United States, Canada, and New Zealand. Local consumption was only about 37,000 tons per year (Sparks, 1997: 642).

Before the creation and the development of the EPZ sector in the 1970s and 1980s, Mauritius had a small industrial sector concentrated on import substitution of basic consumer products, such as food, beverages, tobacco, footwear, and clothing. There was also a fertilizer plant and a refinery to produce ethyl alcohol (ethanol) from molasses (Sparks, 1997).   In order to solve the problem of high level of unemployment and to reduce the dependence on the sugar industry, the Mauritian government adopted in 1971 an outward-looking development strategy based on the EPZ sector.

According to Thomas Meisenhelder (1997), the idea of creating the EPZ sector in Mauritius originated with "a local university professor who was familiar with the experience of Taiwan, and who believed that the East Asian 'tigers' possessed a surplus of capital that could be invested in Mauritius" (Meisenhelder, 1997: 287). Within the EPZ sector, the Mauritian government offers domestic and foreign investors attractive packages of incentives, including tax holidays, exemption from import duties on most raw materials and capital goods, free repatriation of capital, profits and dividends, low-price electricity, etc. About 60 per cent of the capital invested in the EPZ sector was locally owned,   25 per cent owned by Hong Kong entrepreneurs and the remainder supplied mainly by Pakistani, Indian, French, German and British companies (Sparks, 1997). After very slow growth during the 1970s, the Mauritian EPZ rapidly expanded during the 1980s. Describing the tremendous development of the EPZ during this period, Thomas Meisenhelder notes that:

> Designed, subsidised, and guided by the state, the [Mauritian] EPZ expanded annually by as much as 30 per cent in the mid-1980s. By 1990s nearly 600 firms, heavily concentrated in textiles and garments, were employing over 90,000 workers, almost one-third of the island's total work force. They accounted for 63 per cent of all exports and 15 per cent of the gross domestic product, which helps to explain why the overall annual rate of growth during 1983-90 was around 7 per cent. Inflation was not a serious concern and Mauritius had no debt-servicing problem. (Meisenhelder, 1997: 290)

Nevertheless, the growth of the Mauritian EPZ sector slowed down and even declined by the end of the 1980s.   The decline both in new enterprises and employment continued through 1994-1995, when there was only a total of 494 enterprises, employing 82,220 workers, against 591 enterprises, employing 89,669 workers in 1989 (Sparks, 1997; Bowman, 1991).

Mauritius was traditionally an attractive destination for European tourists. However, it was in order to solve the problem of unemployment and reduce the dependence on the sugar production that the Mauritian government decided to develop tourism during the 1970s and 1980s. As a result in the 1990s, tourism became the third most important source of foreign exchange earnings for Mauritius, after the EPZ sector and the sugar industry (Sparks, 1997; Bowman, 1991). Arrivals of tourists increased from 27,650 in 1970 to 400,500 in 1994, and to a record of 422,500 in 1995 (Sparks, 1997). The greatest number of visitors were from France (27.6 per cent), Reunion (18.6 per cent), South Africa (10.1 per cent) and Germany (9.9 per cent). The United Kingdom and Italy were also important markets. According to Donald Sparks (1997), there were plans to expand the number of visitors to 500,000 annually by 2000, but at the same time, the government was implementing measures to curtail and, where possible, reverse the environmental damage caused by the uncontrolled expansion of tourism.

In addition to sugar production, manufacturing in the EPZ sector and tourism, the Mauritian government decided also at the end of the 1980s to promote offshore services as the "fourth pillar" of the economy. However, this new sector was not yet fully developed, and its contribution to the GDP by 1996 was less than 1 per cent of GDP (IMF, 1997b).

The Economic and Social Problems of Mauritius in the 1980s and UNPAAERD

Mauritius was facing a serious economic and social crisis at the end of the 1970s and the beginning of the 1980s. This crisis was characterized by:

- A severe budget deficit,
- Huge deficits of the balance of payments,
- A dramatic increase of external debt, and
- A very high level of unemployment.

Describing the economic crisis facing the country during this period, Larry Bowman underscores the high level of unemployment, which stood at about 15 per cent of the work force (Bowman, 1991: 112), and reports that:

> From 1976 to 1979, Mauritian external debt nearly quadrupled as the government borrowed heavily to meet its import bill and to sustain politically popular government programs. The result was that foreign-exchange reserves, which had stood at $183 million in 1975, fell to just $14 million in August 1979, enough to cover just two weeks of imports. (Bowman, 1991: 118)

In addition, like many other African countries at the beginning of the 1980s, Mauritius also suffered from:

- Falling per capita GNP,[2]
- Relatively high population growth rate,[3] and
- Declining international assistance.[4]

In explaining the Mauritian economic crisis at the end of the 1970s and at the beginning of the 1980s, most analysts pointed to two sets of causes:

1. A set of *underlying causes*, and
2. A set of *direct causes*.

Concerning the *underlying causes*, most analysts (particularly, Bowman, 1991: 103; World Bank, 1989b) argue that Mauritius was handicapped by some structural factors, which included:

- The isolation of the island from the major markets in Western Europe and North America,
- The absence of economies of scale on the island, which limits its capacity of production,
- A heavy dependence on a single export crop (sugar), the price of which fluctuated on the world market; and
- A small economy requiring imports of both food and consumer goods.

The isolation of Mauritius from the major markets (particularly in

Western Europe and North America) has been overcome by the development of modern transportation systems (aerial or maritime), and by the increased economic interests presented by the island for foreign investors and traders. However, it was the small size of the island and its heavy dependence on sugar production that constituted the most important structural problems for Mauritius during the 1970s and 1980s. The small size of the island, or the absence of economies of scale, prevented the development of an industrial sector for the domestic market, which could have created more jobs. In addition, the sugar revenue was not reliable since it depended on the climatic conditions and on the fluctuation of sugar price on the world market (Bowman, 1991; World Bank, 1989b).

With regard to the *direct causes*, these analysts (Bowman, 1991: 103; World Bank, 1989b) emphasized the combination of the following factors:

- The *economic and social policies* adopted by the Seewoosagur Ramgoolam government during the 1970s,
- The sharp *decline of the sugar price* in 1976; and
- The *second oil price shock* in 1979.

In connection with these factors, the World Bank explains the origins of the economic and social problems in Mauritius at the end of the 1970s as follows:

> The [...] reversal in the terms of trade caused by a 23 per cent *decline in sugar prices* in 1976 and the *second oil price shock* in 1979 led to a rapid *deterioration in the balance of payments*, which was further aggravated by the *government's expansionary fiscal stance*. The ensuing *budget deficits* were financed by an increasing recourse to non-concessionary foreign borrowing which caused the *country's external debt* to triple between 1976 and 1979 and the debt-service ratio to increase from a very modest 1 per cent to about 10 per cent. (World Bank, 1989b: 4) (Emphasis added)

Whereas Thomas Meisenhelder (1997) describes the Mauritian economic and social policies of the 1970s as "moderate welfare capitalism," other analysts view them as "expansionary programs" of public-sector investment and social-welfare (Bowman, 1991; World Bank, 1989b). Indeed, in addition to the *Travail pour Tous* ("Work for All") program mentioned earlier, the Mauritian government also initiated at the beginning of the 1970s "several infrastructure projects, including construction of roads, electrical and industrial capacity, and water supply projects" (Bowman, 1991:   117).   Furthermore, it "increased public sector wages faster than the cost of living [...], expanded its efforts in social-welfare areas such as education, health insurance, food subsidies, and pensions" (Bowman, 1991: 117).

All of these programs of public-sector investment and social-welfare were conceived during the favorable economic conditions of the late 1960s and of the beginning of the 1970s, and were mainly financed by tax from the sugar industry. However, by the end of the 1970s, these programs became unsustainable as the sugar price declined and the price of imported goods increased, due particularly to the second oil embargo in 1979 (Bowman, 1991; World Bank, 1989b). As a result, an economic crisis occurred at the end of the 1970s.

Faced with the severe budget deficit and the balance of payments deficits at the end of the 1970s, the Mauritian government had no choice but to seek the assistance of the Bretton Woods institutions, which agreed in 1979 to support Mauritius in exchange for the implementation of an SAP.   This Mauritian SAP is relatively well-known and has been the subject of numerous studies (among many others: Meisenhelder, 1997; Bowman, 1991; Kearney, 1990; World Bank, 1989b). It included the following measures:

- Macroeconomic stabilization,
- Expansion of the EPZ sector,
- Development of tourism,
- Modernization of the sugar industry, and
- Diversification of the agriculture.

As part of the *macroeconomic stabilization,* the Mauritian government was forced to implement measures of austerity, which included the devaluation of its national currency, the reduction of import and government spending, the maintenance of an open market economy, and the promotion of the private sector. In exchange for the acceptance of this austerity package, the Mauritian government received, from 1979 to 1986, about SDR 294.9 million from the IMF, and about $55 million from the World Bank (Bowman, 1991).

With regard to the *expansion of the EPZ sector,* the Mauritian government adopted two important measures in 1983: (1) reduction of the corporate and personal taxes, in order to promote national savings that could be invested in the EPZ sector, and (2) creation of the Mauritius Export Development and Investment Authority (MEDIA), in order to promote EPZ investment and exports around the world (Bowman, 1991).

In order to develop the *tourism sector*, the Mauritian government adopted the following measures: creation of a new airport capable of handling jumbo jets, acquisition of new long-range planes, development of direct flights from major European cities, and encouragement of the construction of new hotels with significant tax incentives for the developers (Bowman, 1991).

At the end of the 1970s, the *sugar industry* was facing tough challenges created by a worldwide overproduction of sugar and a significant growth in the use of artificial sweeteners in most developed countries. These two challenges depressed the world price of sugar to its lowest level in recent years and led to the decline of the real income of the sugar producers. In order to revitalize this sector, the Mauritian government decided in 1985 to modernize it through the implementation of the *Action Plan for the Sugar Industry 1985-1990*, which included the improvement of small planter productivity, the development of scientific research on sugar cane, the reduction of export tax on sugar, and the abolition of all import duties on agricultural equipment and spare parts (Bowman, 1991).

In addition to the modernization of the sugar industry, the Mauritian government decided also to diversify the *agricultural sector*. The goal of this diversification was "to promote other export crops and to augment production for local consumption" (Bowman, 1991). The measures adopted in this domain consisted mainly of developing the tea industry, and improving the production of fruits, vegetables, flowers, and fish.

In evaluating the Mauritian SAP of the 1980s, most analysts recognize the fact that it was implemented, as Larry Bowman (1991: 119) puts it, "with remarkable commitment," and that the results were overwhelmingly positive. As mentioned earlier, most analysts acclaim the economic and social development of Mauritius in the 1980s, resulting from the implementation of this SAP, as an "economic miracle" (Kibazo, March 1996; Duteil, 1993, October 23).

At the macroeconomic level, despite the lack of significant improvement during the period of 1979-1984, the Mauritian economy literally "took off" during the period of 1985-1986, with a GDP growing at the rate of 7.3 per cent in 1985 and 10.1 per cent in 1986.[5]

As a result, the per capita GNP increased from $1110 in 1985 to $1250 in 1986, and to $1620 in 1987. Furthermore, the per capita GNP in 1990 ($2440) reached the double of that of 1979 ($1200).[6] According to the World Bank, by 1992 Mauritius left the group of low-income economies and joined the group of upper-middle-income economies, which included such countries as South Africa, Botswana, Brazil, Mexico, and Malaysia. Most importantly, by this time, Mauritius was no longer under SAP (World Bank, 1994a; 1994b).

Most analysts agree also that the EPZ sector was the engine of the Mauritian economic growth in the 1980s. The EPZ sector grew at about 30 per cent annually during this period. The number of firms operating in this sector jumped from less than 100 firms at the beginning of the 1980s to 586 firms in 1991. During the same period, the number of employees passed from 38,000 to 91,000 (IMF, 1997b: 14). As a result, by the end of 1980s, the EPZ sector became the "major export sector and significant earner of foreign exchange" in Mauritius (Bowman, 1991: 130).

The expansion of tourism was also significant. The number of visitors jumped from an annual average of 100,000 at the beginning of the 1980s to 239,300 in 1988 and 270,000 in 1989. At the same time, the foreign exchange earnings from this sector increased from an annual average of $44 million at the beginning of the 1980s to $177 million in 1988 and $224 million in 1989 (Bowman, 1991).

The development within the agricultural sector was, however, modest. The sugar production stagnated around 600,000 tons annually during the 1980s. By 1989 the sugar industry accounted only for 8 per cent of the GDP (compared to 30 per cent in the 1970s), and for 32 per cent of the total export (compared to 45.9 in 1984). The island became self-sufficient in vegetables, but continued to rely on imports for its main staples (wheat, rice, meat, and dairy products). Furthermore, given the volatility of the world price of tea, the development of the tea industry held no promising future (IMF, 1997b; Bowman, 1991).

In sum, the rigorous implementation of its SAP during the 1980s allowed Mauritius not only to address the pressing problems of budget deficit, balance of payments deficit and increased external debt, but also to create more jobs and revenue through the expansion of the EPZ sector and the development of tourism. Furthermore, the SAP made Mauritius very attractive to ODA and FDI. In the case of Mauritius, the implementation of UNPAAERD would not have solved any of these economic and social problems. On the contrary, it would have exacerbated them.

Like Madagascar and many other African countries, Mauritius was already implementing its SAP with the Bretton Woods institutions, when the UN General Assembly adopted UNPAAERD in 1986. Also like Madagascar and other African countries, Mauritius did not oppose the adoption of this development program, nor did it try to implement it. Therefore, in order to understand the potential failure of UN-PAAERD with respect to Mauritius, we have to discuss whether it could have been used to solve the economic and social problems of this country at the end of the 1970s and at the beginning of the 1980s.

Referring to the measures contained in UNPAAERD, we have to recognize that these measures would not have solved the Mauritian economic and social problems at the end of the 1970s and at the beginning of the 1980s. First, to begin with the urgent problems of budget deficit, balance of payments deficits, and external debt, although UNPAAERD contained some measures related to the so-called "policy reforms," its main focus was in reality on the development of agriculture and other sectors in support of agriculture.[7] Besides, as we found in the case of Madagascar, only an agreement with the Bretton Woods institutions on the implementation of an SAP could solve these problems. Therefore, since the Bretton Woods institutions did not support UNPAAERD and the UN General Assembly could not play the role of these institutions, Mauritius could never have solved its macroeconomic problems, if it tried to implement the UN development program without an agreement with the Bretton Woods institutions on the implementation of an SAP.

Second, the implementation of its SAP led Mauritius to adopt an outward-looking development strategy based on the expansion of the EPZ sector and the development of tourism. This outward-looking development strategy also allowed the country to create more jobs and revenue, and to attract more ODA and FDI. The implementation of UNPAAERD, which would have led the country to embrace an inward-looking development strategy, would never have produced the same results as the SAP. This is because UNPAAERD's inward-looking development strategy, which was aimed at the achievement of food self-reliance and self-sufficiency, would have been automatically limited by the small size of the country. In other words, by adopting UNPAAERD's inward-looking development strategy, Mauritius would not have produced more than what its tiny national market could have absorbed, nor more that what its limited national resources could have allowed.   Consequently, if UNPAAERD had been implemented in Mauritius, the country would have completely missed its economic miracle of the 1980s, which was built on an outward-looking development strategy that was based particularly on the expansion of the EPZ sector and the development of tourism.

Thus, in the case of Mauritius, it is clear that UNPAAERD was totally useless in addressing the specific economic and social problems of this country at the end of the 1970s and at the beginning of the 1980s. In fact, only an agreement with the Bretton Woods institutions and a rigorous implementation of an SAP could have allowed this country to solve successfully these problems and to achieve at the same time an "economic miracle."

The Economic and Social Problems of Mauritius in the 1990s and UNNADAF

Compared to many African countries, which continued to endure critical economic and social conditions, Mauritius was a relatively prosperous country at the beginning of the 1990s. Indeed, its GDP grew by an average of 7.7 per cent a year during the period of 1985-1989, and its citizens enjoyed a per capita GNP of $2,430 in 1990, compared respectively to an average GDP growth rate of 2.5 per cent and an average per capita GNP of $674 for all Africa (World Bank, 2001). In addition, while the country continued to depend on food imports, there was no risk of famine or hunger (as there was in many other African countries), because there was no serious balance of payments deficits. The population growth rate remained at the low level of 1.3 per cent (compared to 2.6 per cent a year for the whole continent) (World Bank, 1997a: 7). Furthermore, while the external debt continued to increase, the Mauritian debt-GDP ratio remained relatively low (17 per cent compared to 94 per cent for the whole continent) (World Bank, 1997a: 180). The ODA was also declining, but the country was still in good financial condition as the gross domestic investment and the FDI remained high.

In fact, the major concern of the Mauritian government at the beginning of the 1990s was the relative decline of the GDP growth rates, which dropped from the annual average of 7.7 per cent during the period of 1985-1989 to 5.5 per cent during the period of 1990-1992 (IMF, 1997b, 1996).[8] According to most analysts, this problem was due to the stagnation followed by the decline of the EPZ sector (IMF,

1997b, 1996; Bowman, 1991). Indeed, after having reached nearly 600 in 1988, the number of firms operating in the EPZ sector stagnated at this level, and started to decline at the beginning of the 1990s (IMF, 1997b and 1996).

In explaining the causes of this decline of the EPZ sector, the IMF points to the progressive "loss of competitiveness" of Mauritius compared with other countries in Asia, Eastern Europe and Latin America, which have adopted similar development strategies (IMF, 1997b and 1996). This loss of competitiveness was due to the succession of wage increases and the lack of qualified labor force in Mauritius. According to the IMF, the succession of wage increases in the Mauritian EPZ sector since the early 1990s have been "out of line with labor productivity, thus driving up unit labor costs by more than 50 per cent between 1990 and 1995" (IMF, 1997b: 14). In addition, the "lack of an adequately qualified labor force with the necessary skills to operate an increasingly sophisticated technology" constrained investment and growth in the Mauritian EPZ sector (IMF, 1997b: 14).

In order to regain the high GDP growth rates of the 1980s, the Mauritian government decided to revitalize the EPZ sector by adopting different measures, which consisted in consolidating and diversifying this sector. At the same time, in order to attract more investment and more firms, the Mauritian government decided also to promote the offshore services (IMF, 1997b and 1996).

With regard to the consolidation of the EPZ sector, the government provided incentives to allow firms operating in this sector to "invest heavily in plant and machinery and gradually reduce its work force with a view to increasing productivity and moving to higher value-added products" (IMF, 1997b: 14). In addition, since the EPZ sector was dominated by textiles and wearing apparel, the Mauritian government also decided to diversify this sector by "promoting investments in nontextile industries, including plastics, leather, jewelry, computer software, electronics, and pharmaceuticals" (IMF, 1997b: 14).

In order to further diversify the economy and to attract more investment and international firms, the Mauritian government decided to launch in 1989 the offshore services. These offshore services started with banking activities and extended to a freeport and other types of nonbanking activities, including offshore fund management, royalties companies, operational headquarters, construction, securities, consultancy companies, ship management, trading, and "reinvoincing"

(IMF, 1997b, 1996; Craig, March 23, 1992).

In assessing the development policies adopted by the Mauritian government at the beginning of the 1990s, most analysts concluded that the results were generally positive. Despite the fact that Mauritius did not regain the high GDP growth rates of the second half of the 1980s, these new development policies allowed the country to maintain relatively high GDP growth rates averaging 5 per cent a year during the period of 1996-1999, compared to 2.4 per cent for all Africa (World Bank, 2001: 15). As a result, the per capita GNP in Mauritius increased from an average of $3050 during the period of 1991-1995 to $3665 during the period of 1996-1999, while the per capita GNP for all Africa only increased from an average of $679 to $695 during the same periods (World Bank, 2001: 33).

Particularly, concerning the consolidation of the EPZ sector, the IMF reported that, "between 1991 and 1995, the number of EPZ firms declined by almost 18 percent, from 586 units to 481, and the number of employees by more than 11 percent, from about 91,000 to nearly 80,500" (IMF, 1997b: 14). However, according to the IMF, these contractions have been compensated by "an increase in investment for plant and machinery (as well as management techniques)" (IMF, 1997b: 14).

The diversification of the EPZ sector seemed to have been more successful than its consolidation. Indeed, according to the IMF,

> between 1991 and 1995, employment in the nontextile EPZ companies has increased by about 10 percent, from slightly less than 9,400 to about 10,300 persons. During the same period, exports of this subsector grew by almost 71 percent [...], while those of the textile sector grew at a slower pace: a cumulative 46 percent. (IMF, 1997b: 14).

With regard to the offshore services, the IMF reports that the Mauritius Freeport, which was officially set up in 1992, was operating, providing for "pure trading and transshipment operations as well as minor processing, simple assembly and repackaging" (IMF, 1997b: 17). In addition, by 1996, 7 offshore banks and about 4,300 offshore nonbanking companies were operating on the island (IMF, 1997b: 18; Craig, March 23, 1992). Nevertheless, the real impacts of these offshore services on the Mauritian economy were still limited. According to the IMF (1997b), while the total trade passing through the freeport (i.e., imports plus exports) has increased since 1993, the freeport's direct contribution to the Mauritian GDP was estimated to less than 0.1 per cent of the GDP. The contribution of other offshore services was even smaller.

Mauritius was implementing its new development policies when the UN General Assembly adopted UNNADAF in 1991. Just as in 1986 with UNPAAERD, Mauritius did not oppose the adoption of this new UN development program, nor did it try to implement it. However, in order to understand the potential failure of UNNADAF with respect to the case of Mauritius, we need to discuss whether it could have been used to solve the economic and social problems of this country in the 1990s.

Referring to the measures contained in UNNADAF, it is clear that these measures would never have helped Mauritius to sustain such high GDP growth rates during the 1990s. On the contrary, the implementation of this UN development program in the 1990s would have provoked disastrous economic and social consequences in the country.

UNNADAF did not contain any measure equivalent to the consolidation and diversification of the EPZ sector, which were in line with the outward-looking development strategy adopted by Mauritius since the end of 1970s. In reality, UNNADAF was based on an inward-looking development strategy, focusing on import-substituting industrialization (ISI), which was diametrically opposed to the Mauritian development strategy. While the Mauritian development strategy was the source of the economic miracle of this country in the 1980s, the inward-looking development strategy prescribed by UNNADAF has been tried in many other countries (especially in Latin America), and has consistently failed (Spero and Hart, 1997; Rapley, 1996; Cox, 1987). Therefore, if UNNADAF had been implemented in Mauritius in the 1990s, it would have automatically failed, and would have ruined the successful economy of this country by destroying its main engine, which was the EPZ sector.

Furthermore, the concept of "offshore services" was entirely alien to UNNADAF. In fact, given the inward-looking development strategy they have adopted, the designers of UNNADAF would have discouraged, if not condemned, the promotion of the Mauritian offshore services, which contributed to the economic development of the country by training workers, creating jobs, and renting lands and facilities (Thompson, 2002; IMF, 1997b). Although their contribution to the Mauritian GDP was rather limited by the end of the 1990s, they certainly provided a new dimension to the Mauritian economy. Consequently, the implementation of UNNADAF would have deprived the Mauritian economy of this new dimension.

In sum, in the case of Mauritius, UNNADAF would not have helped to sustain high GDP growth rates in the 1990s. On the contrary, the implementation of this UN development program would have completely ruined the Mauritian economy by destroying the EPZ sector and by depriving it of its new dimension provided by the offshore services.

Conclusion

The case of Mauritius clearly demonstrates that UNPAAERD and UNNADAF were useless for addressing the specific economic and social problems of this country in the 1980s and 1990s. On the contrary, if they were implemented in this country, these two UN development programs would have provoked disastrous economic and social consequences. Thus, the Mauritian government had good reasons for not implementing these programs, even if it did not oppose their adoption by the UN General Assembly.

Particularly, with regard to UNPAAERD, the implementation of this program would not have solved the problems of budget deficit, balance of payments deficits, and external debt faced by Mauritius at the end of the 1970s and at the beginning of the 1980s. Only an agreement with the Bretton Woods institutions and the implementation of an SAP could have helped Mauritius to solve these problems and at the same time achieve an economic miracle. In this case, the implementation of UNPAAAERD would have aggravated the economic and social problems of Mauritius instead of solving them.

Furthermore, the implementation of UNNADAF would never have helped Mauritius to sustain high GDP growth rates in the 1990s. On the contrary, the implementation of this UN development program would have distracted this country from its successful outward-looking development strategy, and would have completely ruined its economy by destroying the EPZ sector and by depriving it of its new dimension provided by the offshore services.

Notes

[1] Fig. 7.1 – Mauritius: GDP Growth Rates (1975-1999), below, p. 129, and Fig. 7.2 – Mauritius: Per Capita GNP (1975-1999), below, p. 130.

[2] According to the World Bank, the per capita GNP for Mauritius fell from $1260 in 1981 to $1080 in 1984 (World bank, 2001: 33). See Fig. 7.1 – Mauritius: GDP Growth Rates (1975-1999), below, p. 129, and Fig. 7.2 Mauritius: Per Capita GNP (1975-1999), below, p. 130.

[3] According to the World Bank, the average annual growth rate of the Mauritian population during the period 1980-1985 was 1.2 per cent (World Bank, 1995: 7). This is relatively low compared to the annual growth rate of 2.9 per cent for all Africa, and 3.0 per cent for sub-Saharan Africa. However, given the small size of the island and the acute problem of unemployment at the beginning of the 1980s, this population growth rate of 1.2 per cent caused a lot of concerns for the Mauritian government.

[4] According to the World Bank, the net official ODA to Mauritius declined, in current prices, from $69 million in 1980 to $27 million in 1985, despite the fact that there was an increase to $94 million in 1981 (World bank, 1995: 315).

[5] See Fig. 7.1 – Mauritius: GDP Growth Rates (1975-1999), below, p. 129, and Fig. 7.2 – Mauritius: Per Capita GNP (1975-1999), below, p. 130.

[6] *Ibid.*.

[7] UN document A/RES/S-13/2 of 01 June 1986, annex II.A.1.e. See the analysis of UNPAAERD in Chapter 3.

[8] See Fig. 7.1 – Mauritius: GDP Growth Rates (1975-1999), below, p. 129.

Chapter 8

Conclusion

The failure of UNPAAERD and UNNADAF in the 1980s and 1990s can be explained by the combined effects of *internal* and *external causes,* which have been identified through the systematic analyses of the two programs, and by taking into consideration the late 20th century world economic order. The study of the cases of Madagascar and Mauritius concretized these analyses and demonstrated that the two UN development programs were useless in dealing with the specific economic and social problems of these countries. In other words, it was the conjunction of the *institutional weaknesses* of the UN organization itself, and the constraints imposed upon these programs by the *interacting forces within the late 20th century world economic order* that led to the failure of these two UN development programs. The *institutional weaknesses* of the UN included its inability to generate potentially effective development programs and to get the compliance of all members of the international community. And the capitalist material capabilities, the variants of liberal ideas and the Bretton Woods institutions constituted the *interacting forces within the late 20th century world economic order.*

The systematic analyses of UNPAAERD and UNNADAF in Chapters 2, 3, and 4, demonstrated that the failure of these programs stemmed from the application of the structuralist theory and/or dependency theory in interpreting the causes of the critical economic and social conditions in Africa in the 1980s and 1990s. The application of these theories led the African political leaders and policy makers to identify wrong problems and prescribe inappropriate solutions. They arrived at the conclusion that the most important obstacles to economic and social development on the continent were the lack of structural transformation (i.e., lack of industrialization) of the African economies, their dependence of on the world economy, and that vulnerability to external shocks.

As a result of this interpretation, the African political leaders and policy makers, who strongly influenced the formulation of the two UN development programs, prescribed an inward-looking development strategy based on the unrealistic goal and strategy of *collective self-reliance*. In its application in UNPAAERD, this interpretation led to the adoption of measures for the development of agriculture and the sectors in support of agriculture in order to achieve agricultural and food self-sufficiency and self-reliance.   And in its application in UNNADAF, it led to the adoption of measures for import-substituting industrialization (ISI), and measures for regional cooperation and integration.

An appropriate interpretation of the causes of the critical economic and social conditions in Africa in the 1980s and 1990s would have revealed, however, that the lack of structural transformation of the African economies, their dependence on the world economy, and their vulnerability to external shocks were not the main causes of these critical conditions.   On the contrary, as discussed in Chapter 4, many African countries were in fact trapped in protracted armed conflicts and/or political instability for many years, and had no hope of achieving sustainable development unless peace and stability were reestablished.   Other African countries were ruined by economic mismanagement or inappropriate economic policies, if they were not simply plundered by "predatory kleptocrat" political leaders.   These countries had no prospects to develop unless appropriate economic policies were adopted, or peaceful democratic processes would take place and would allow to get rid of these predatory political leaders. Still other African countries were handicapped by serious deterioration of the environment or permanent droughts, and could not develop without fundamental economic and social transformations, which may involve changing the way of life of many people.

The flaws in the processes of policy formulation, recommendation, and adoption within the UN General Assembly allowed the adoption of UNPAAERD and UNNADAF by the world organization despite their potential ineffectiveness. Indeed, the only criterion of recommendation and adoption that has been used, was the *responsiveness* of these programs to the priorities set by the African countries. Consequently, there was no serious consideration of other alternative development programs, and the UN General Assembly simply adopted the African proposals, whether they were potentially effective or not. In other words, the processes of policy recommendation and adoption within the UN General Assembly simply did not lead to the adoption of the most potentially effective development programs. These "intellectual and organizational limits" of the UN organization (Puchala, 1996), also described as "institutional weaknesses" by some analysts (Gwin and Williams, 1996), characterized by the flaws in the processes of policy formulation, recommendation, and adoption, explain to a large extent the failure of the two UN development programs.

The implementation of the two UN development programs was also seriously handicapped by the non-compliance of virtually all member states and all international organizations, which resulted in the lack of policy inputs and processes in their implementation. The financial resources from the international donors and the African countries themselves did not come forth as expected. Besides, the implementation of the two UN development programs was based on the concept of *global compact*, which means that the African countries and the international community were committed to take actions as specified in these programs. However, this approach led to the fact that no specific entity (individual or organization) was designated to administer the two programs. Nobody was directly responsible for their implementation, and nobody was in control of the policy inputs and processes required for their implementation.

Finally, with regard to the processes of evaluation, the UN General Assembly was unable to evaluate rigorously and accurately its own development programs. This inaccurate evaluation did not contribute to the identification of the major causes of the failure of the first program, and did not lead to any improvement in the formulation and implementation of the second one. Consequently, the same mistakes were made in the formulation and implementation of the two UN development programs. Particularly, the two programs suffered from the lack of available financial resources and the lack of administrator. They were also based on the same concept of *global compact*, and aimed at the same unrealistic goal of *collective self-reliance*.

Concerning the external causes of failure, it was obvious that the authors of UNPAAERD and UNNADAF did not follow the constraints of the interacting forces within the late 20th century world economic order. These interacting forces, consisting of capitalist material capabilities, different currents of liberal ideas, and the Bretton Woods institutions, decisively contributed to the failure of these two UN development programs.

First, contrary to the prescriptions of the two UN development programs, the capitalist material capabilities of the late 20th century world economic order compelled most African countries to embrace capitalism, open up their economy to international trade and foreign investment, and adopt an outward-looking strategy in order to avoid economic instability and marginalization from the world economy. By following these constraints, they were automatically compelled to abandoned the two UN development programs, which prescribed a distributive and closed economic system, and an inward-looking development strategy based on the concept of collective *self-reliance.*

Second, the domination of liberal ideas in the late 20th century also constrained the African countries to embrace the basic elements of liberalism associated with capitalism and democracy, which included individual freedom, individual entrepreneurship, sovereignty of the market, and reduced role of the state and the public sector in the economy. The adoption of these liberal ideas also compelled the African countries to abandon the two UN development programs, which promoted ideas related to collectivism, distributive economic system, and substantial state intervention in the economy.

Finally, the powerful constraints of the Bretton Woods institutions decisively compelled the African countries to adopt structural adjustment programs (SAPs), which included macroeconomic stabilization, price liberalization, and reduced role of the state and the public sector in the economy. The adoption of these SAPs led them also to abandon the two UN development programs, which were not supported neither by the Bretton Woods institutions nor by the capitalist developed countries, did not help them to borrow money from the global financial market, and to attract more official development assistance (ODA) and foreign direct investment (FDI).

The study of the cases of Madagascar and Mauritius demonstrated that UNPAAERD and UNNADAF were totally useless in dealing with the specific economic and social problems of these two African countries in the 1980s and 1990s. In fact, instead of solving the economic and social problems of these countries, the two UN development programs would have aggravated them.

The case of Madagascar showed that this country adopted in the 1970s an inward-looking development strategy based on the socialist concepts of autonomous development, self-sufficiency, and self-reliance. This development strategy was very similar to the OAU's development strategy contained in the *Lagos Plan of Action*, which was based on the concept of "*collective self-reliance*," and strongly influenced the formulation of both UNPAAERD and UNNADAF. In connection of its development strategy, Madagascar adopted different measures of nationalization of the economy and, particularly, a program of investment known as *investissement à outrance* ("investment to the extreme limit"). However, the implementation of these measures resulted in a total disruption of the economy and to the loss of the creditworthiness of the country at the beginning of the 1980s. It was only the adoption of SAP with the Bretton Woods institutions, which saved the Malagasy economy from a total collapse in 1982. Nevertheless, the economic recovery of the country was disrupted by a persistent political instability and the reluctance of most political leaders to pursue the implementation of the SAP until 1996.

Therefore, in the case of Madagascar, the implementation of UNPAAERD in the 1980s and UNNADAF in the 1990s would not have solved the economic and social problems of the country. None of these UN development programs would have contributed to the recovery of the creditworthiness of this country, or would have attracted more ODA and more domestic and foreign investment. On the contrary, the implementation of these two UN development programs would have led Madagascar to repeat the same mistakes it made in the 1970s, and would have aggravated the economic and social problems of this country.

Mauritius adopted at independence a "moderate welfare capitalism," which became unsustainable in the context of declining sugar price and increasing oil price at the end of the 1970s. As in the case of Madagascar, the adoption of an SAP with the Bretton Woods institutions was the only viable solution for the economic recovery of the country at the end of the 1970s. The consistent implementation of this SAP, which included reduction of budget deficit, modernization of the sugar industry, expansion of the Export Processing Zone (EPZ) sector, and development of tourism, allowed Mauritius to achieve its "economic miracle" in the second half of the 1980s. At the beginning of the 1990s, the major problem of this country was the declining growth rates of its GDP. By this time, the viable solutions were constituted by further liberalization and diversification of the economy, and the promotion of offshore services.

The case of Mauritius clearly demonstrated that the two UN development programs, based on an inward-looking development strategy, would not have solved the specific economic and social problems of this country. On the contrary, the implementation of these programs would have provoked disastrous economic and social consequences. Indeed, in the 1980s, UNPAAERD, which focused on the development of the agricultural sector, would not have resolved the problems related to budget deficit, balance of payments deficits, and unemployment in Mauritius. Instead, it would have aggravated these problems. Furthermore, at the beginning of the 1990s, UNNADAF, which focused on import-substituting industrialization (ISI), and on regional cooperation and integration, would not have solved the problems related to the declining growth rates of GDP. On the contrary, it would have provoked a disruption of the Mauritius economy, which was based on an outward-looking development strategy, and was driven by the EPZ sector and tourism.

If the approach and the conclusions of this study are correct, it should be possible to make some suggestions on how to improve the formulation and implementation of international development programs through the UN organization (or another international development organization). There are three major suggestions that need to be emphasized in order to make an international development program more effective: first, an international development program should be designed for a specific country, not for a whole continent (or even for a group of countries); second, it should not only be accepted by the political leaders of the country, but also approved and supported by the international donors; third, it should be embedded in the prevailing world economic order.

One of the major flaws in UNPAAERD and UNNADAF was that the designers of these two UN development programs assumed that all African countries had the same problems and, therefore, had to adopt the same prescriptions. According to these policy makers, the main cause of the critical economic and social conditions in Africa in the 1980s and 1990s was the lack of structural transformation (i.e., lack of industrialization), which would have led to the dependence of African economies and their vulnerability to external shocks. Therefore, the main solution would be to achieve *collective self-reliance and self-sufficiency* in agricultural and food production through the implementation of UNPAAERD in the 1980s, and to achieve *collective self-reliance and self-sufficiency* in industrial production through the implementation of UNNADAF in the 1990s.

This study revealed, however, that even though the lack of

industrialization, the dependence of the African economies, and their vulnerability to external shocks may have existed, the economic and social problems of all African countries were not necessarily the same. Consequently, they should not have adopted the same development programs. The cases of Madagascar and Mauritius demonstrated, for instance, that while both countries depended on the export of primary products in the 1970s (vanilla and coffee for Madagascar; sugar for Mauritius), and faced similar problems of budget deficit and balance of payments deficits, the causes of these problems were not the same. Consequently, these countries had to adopt different types of SAPs that specifically addressed these problems. In the case of Madagascar, in addition to macroeconomic stabilization, the most important measures which sparked the economic activities in this country in the 1980s were the liberalization of the economy and the privatization of the state-owned enterprises. In the case of Mauritius, the economic recovery and development in the 1980s were achieved through macroeconomic stabilization, modernization of the sugar industry, expansion of the Export Procession Zone (EPZ) sector and development of tourism. This is why a potentially effective development program should be *country-specific*. It should take into consideration the specific political, economic, and social problems of the country for which it is designed, along with the specific resources (natural, human, financial, etc.) that can be used in the development of the country. Short of such specificity, any development program is doomed to fail.

Second, this study also demonstrated that the acceptance of a given development program by the political leaders of a given country and the approval and support of such development program by the international donors constituted two major conditions for its effectiveness. On the one hand, it is obvious that no development program could be implemented in any country, if the political leaders of that country refused to implement it. The case of Madagascar at the beginning of the 1990s clearly showed that, even if the SAP was producing some positive results, the reluctance of most political leaders to continue its implementation automatically killed this program. On the other hand, the sustainability of a development program in a given developing country also depends on its approval and support by the international donors, particularly the Bretton Woods institutions and the capitalist developed countries. The cases of the two UN development programs clearly demonstrated that the lack of support from these international donors, which resulted in the lack of financial resources, was one of the major causes of the failure of these programs.

Finally, this study also demonstrated that another major cause of the failure of the two UN development programs was the fact that they were running against the prevailing world economic order. As mentioned earlier, the authors of UNPAAERD and UNNADAF did not follow the constraints imposed by the interacting forces within the late 20th century world economic order. Most of the important measures included in these two UN development programs were inappropriate within this prevailing world economic order. Whereas the interacting forces within this world economic order required an outward-looking development strategy, which was embedded in the growing global economy and increasing economic interdependence among all countries in the world, the two UN development programs prescribed an inward-looking development strategy, which has already failed in Africa and other developing continents. Consequently, the implementation of these programs would have aggravated the lack of competitiveness of the African economies and their further marginalization within the world economy. In fact, the cases of Madagascar and Mauritius clearly showed that it was only within the prevailing world economic order, based on capitalist material capabilities, liberal ideas and the Bretton Woods institutions, that economic and social development could occur in Africa.

Bibliography

Adams, Nassau. (1994). "The UN's Neglected Brief -- 'The Advancement of All Peoples'?" in Childers, Erskine (Ed.) (1994). *Challenges to the United Nations: Building a Safer World*. London: Catholic Institute for International Relations; New York: St. Martin's Press, pp. 26-50.

Ajaegbo, D. I. (1986). "First Development Decade, 1960-1970: The United Nations and the Economic Development of Africa," *Transafrican Journal of History*, No. 15, pp. 1-17.

_____. (1984 and 1985). "The United Nations Development Decade in Africa, 1960- 1970: A Political and Socio-Cultural Analysis," *Journal of Eastern African Research and Development*, No. 14 (1984), pp. 1-18; and No. 15 (1985), pp. 112-146.

Allen, Philip M. (1997). *Madagascar: Conflicts of Authority in the Great Island*. Boulder, San Francisco, Oxford: Westview Press.

Alter, Rolf (1991). "Lessons from the Export Processing Zone in Mauritius," in *Finance and Development*, Vol. 28, N. 4, pp. 7-9.

Amin, Samir (1967). *Le Developpement du Capitalism en Cote d' Ivoire*. Paris: Editions de Minuit.

_____. (1976). *Unequal Development*. New York: Monthly Review Press.

Archer, Robert (1976). *Madagascar Depuis 1972: La Marche d' une Revolution*. Paris: L' Harmattan.

Ayittey, George B. N. (July 26, 1996). "The UN's Shameful Record in Africa," in *The Wall Street Journal*, Section A, p. 12.

"Bad Guy Makes Good," in *The Economist* (March, 22, 1997), Vol. 342, No. 8009, p. 51.

Baldwin, David A. (1993). "Neoliberalism, Neorealism, and World Politics," in Baldwin, David A. (Ed.) *Neorealism and Neoliberalism: The Contemporary Debate*. New York: Columbia University Press, pp. 3-25.

_____. (Ed.) (1993). *Neorealism and Neoliberalism: The Contemporary Debate*. New York: Columbia University Press.

156   *The Failure of the UN Development Programs for Africa*

Bannock, Graham et al. (Eds.) (1987). *Dictionary of Economics*. New Edition. London: Penguin Group.

Barnet, Richard J. and Cavanagh, John (1994). *Global Dreams: Imperial Corporations and the New World Order*. New York: Touchstone.

Barro, Robert J. (1997). *The Determinants of Economic Growth*. Cambridge (Massachusetts); London: The MIT Press.

Berg, Elliot (1986). "The World Bank's Strategy," in Ravenhill, John (Ed.) (1986). *Africa in Economic Crisis*. New York: Columbia University Press, pp. 44-59.

Blomstrom, Magnus and Mats Lundahl (Eds.) (1993). *Economic Crisis in Africa: Perspectives on Policy Responses*. London and New York: Routledge.

Bowman, Larry W. (1991). *Mauritius: Democracy and Development in the Indian Ocean*. Boulder and San Francisco: Westview Press; London: Dartmouth.

Brown, Mervyn (1997). "Madagascar: Recent History," in *Africa South of the Sahara 1997*, 36th Edition, London: Europa Publications Ltd., pp. 564- 569.

Callaghy, Thomas M. (1995). "Africa and the World Political Economy: Still Caught Between a Rock and a Hard Place," in Harbeson, John W. and Rothchild, Donald (Eds.) *Africa in World Politics: Post-Cold War Challenges*. Boulder, San Francisco, Oxford: Westview Press, pp. 41-68.

Cardoso, Fernando and Faletto, Enzo (1979). *Dependency and Development in Latin America*. Translated by Marjory Mattingly Urquidi. Berkeley: University of California Press.

Childers, Erskine (1994). *Renewing the United Nations System*. Uppsala, Sweden: Dag Hammarskjold Foundation.

Childers, Erskine (Ed.) (1994). *Challenges to the United Nations: Building a Safer World*. London: Catholic Institute for International Relations; New York: St. Martin's Press.

Collingsworth, Terry, J. William Goold, and Pharis F. Harvey (1994). "Time for a Global New Deal: Labor and Free Trade." *Foreign Affairs*, Vol. 73, No. 1, pp. 8-14.

Cornia, Giovanni A. and Gerald K. Helleiner (Eds.) (1994). *From Adjustment to Development in Africa: Conflict, Controversy, Convergence, Consensus?* New York: St. Martin's Press.

Covell, Maureen (1987). *Madagascar: Politics, Economics and Society*. London and New York: Frances Pinter.

Cox, Robert W. (1993a). "Gramsci, Hegemony and International Relations: An Essay in Method," in Gill, Stephen (Ed.) (1993). *Gramsci, Historical Materialism and International Relations*. New York: Cambridge University Press, pp. 49-66.

_____. (1993b). "Structural Issues of Global Governance: Implications for Europe," in Gill, Stephen (Ed.) (1993). *Gramsci, Historical*

Materialism and International Relations. New York: Cambridge University Press, pp. 259-289.

_____. (1987). *Production, Power, and World Order: Social Forces in the Making of History*. New York: Columbia University Press.

_____. (1986). "Social Forces, States and World Orders: Beyond International Relations Theory," revised version in Keohane, Robert O. (Ed.). *Neorealism and its Critics*. New York: Columbia University Press, pp. 204-254. (This article was initially published in *Millenium*, Vol. 10 (1981), pp. 127-155).

_____. (1979). "Ideologies and the New International Economic Order: Reflections on Some Recent Literature," in *International Organization*, Vol. 33, No. 2, pp. 257- 302. (This article is reprinted in Cox, Robert W. with Sinclair, Timothy J., 1996, pp. 376- 419).

Cox, Robert W. with Sinclair, Timothy J. (1996). *Approaches to World Order*. New York: Cambridge University Press.

Craig, Peter (March 23, 1992). "Mauritius, a Success Story of the 1980s, is Looking for Investors to Participate in the Next Development Phase," in *Business America*, Vol. 113, No. 6, p. 28.

Crossette, B. (March 17, 1996). "UN, World Bank and IMF Join $25 Billion Drive for Africa," *The New York Times* (Sunday), p. 6.

Danaher, Kevin (Ed.) (1994). *50 Years is Enough: The Case Against the World Bank and the International Monetary Fund*. Boston: South End Press

Decalo, Samuel (1992). "The Process, Prospects and Constraints of Democratization in Africa," *African Affairs*, No. 91, pp. 7-35

DeLancey, Mark W. (1994). "The New Role of the UN and the Third World: The Sub-Saharan Africa Case," in Ra, Jong Yil (Ed.) (1994). *The New World Order and the Role of the UN*. Korea: Ye-Jin Press, pp. 279-305.

DeLancey, Mark W., et al. (1997). *African International Relations: An Annotated Bibliography*, 2nd Edition, Boulder, Colorado; and Oxford: Westview Press.

DeLancey, Mark and Mays, T.M. (1994). *Historical Dictionary of International Organizations in Sub-Saharan Africa*, Metuchen, New Jersey and London: The Scarecrow Press, Inc.

Deleris, Ferdinand (1986). *Ratsiraka: Socialisme et Misère à Madagascar*. Paris: L' Harmattan.

Demery, Lionel (1994). "Structural Adjustment: Its Origins, Rationale and Achievements," in Cornia, G. A. and Helleiner, G. K. (Eds.) *From Adjustment to Development in Africa: Conflicts, Controversy, Convergence, Consensus?* New York: St. Martin's Press, pp. 25-48.

Deschamps, Hubert (1972). *Histoire de Madagascar*. Paris: Berger-Levrault.

Dorosh, Paul and Bernier, Rene (1994). "Staggered Reforms and Limited Success: Structural Adjustment in Madagascar," in Sahn, David E. (Ed.) (1994). *Adjusting to Policy Failure in African Economies*.

Ithaca and London: Cornell University Press, pp. 332-365.

Dougherty, James E. and Pfaltzgraff, Robert L. Jr., (1990). Contending Theories of International Relations: A Comprehensive Survey. 3rd edition. New York: Harper Collins Publishers.

Dunn, William N. (1994). *Public Policy Analysis: An Introduction.* Englewood Cliffs, New Jersey: Prentice Hall.

Duruflé, Gilles (1989). "Structural Disequilibria and Adjustment Programmes in Madagascar," in Campbell, B. K. (Ed.). *Structural Adjustment in Africa.* New York: St. Martin's Press, pp169-201.

Duteil, M. (October 23, 1993). "Maurice, L' Ile du Miracle," in *Le Point,* No. 1101, pp. 22- 24.

Easterly, William and Ross Levine (1997). "Africa's Growth Tragedy: Policies and Ethnic Divisions," in *The Quarterly Journal of Economics* (November 1997), pp. 1203- 1250.

Engberg-Pedersen, Poul, Peter Gibbon, Phil Raikes and Lars Udsholt (1996). *Limits of Adjustment in Africa: The Effects of Economic Liberalization, 1986-94.* Copenhagen: Centre for Development Research; Oxford: James Currey; Portsmouth, NH: Heinemann.

Findlay, Ronald and Wellisz, Stanislaw (1993a). "Introduction," in Findlay, Ronald and Wellisz, Stanislaw (Eds.) (1993). *Five Small Open Economies.* New York, NY: Oxford University Press, pp. 1-15.

_____. (1993b). "The Comparative Study," in Findlay, Ronald and Wellisz, Stanislaw (Eds.) (1993). *Five Small Open Economies.* New York, NY: Oxford University Press, pp. 293-322.

Findlay, Ronald and Wellisz, Stanislaw (Eds.) (1993). *Five Small Open Economies.* New York, NY: Oxford University Press.

Fosu, Augustin K. (1992). "Political Instability and Economic Growth: Evidence from Sub-Saharan Africa," in *Economic Development and Cultural Change,* Vol. XL (1992), pp. 829- 841.

Frank, Andre Gunder (1967). *Capitalism and Underdevelopment in Latin America.* New York: Monthly Review Press.

Fredland, Richard (1990). *A Guide to African International Organizations.* London, Melbourne, Munich, New York: Hans Zell Publishers.

Gill, Stephen (1991). "Historical Materialism, Gramsci, and International Political Economy," in Murphy, Craig and Tooze, R. (Eds.) (1991). *The New International Political Economy.* Boulder, Colorado: Lynne Rienner Publishers, pp. 51-76.

Gill, Stephen (1993a). "Gramsci and Global Politics: Towards a Post-Hegemonic Research Agenda," in Gill, Stephen (Ed.) *Gramsci, Historical Materialism and International Relations.* New York: Cambridge University Press, pp. 1-18.

_____. (1993b). "Epistemology, Ontology and the 'Italian School'," Gill, Stephen (Ed.) *Gramsci, Historical Materialism and International Relations.* New York: Cambridge University Press, pp. 21-48.

_____. (1990). *American Hegemony and the Trilateral Commission.* New

York: Cambridge University Press .

Gill, Stephen (Ed.) (1993). *Gramsci, Historical Materialism and International Relations.* New York: Cambridge University Press.

Goulet, Denis (1977). *The Cruel Choice: A New Concept in the Theory of Development.* New York: Atheneum.

Gow, Bonar A. (1997). "Admiral Didier Ratsiraka and the Malagasy Socialist Revolution," in *The Journal of Modern African African Studies,* Vol. 35, No. 3, pp. 409-439.

Griffin, Michael. (May-June, 1987). "Ratsiraka's Volte-Face." *Africa Report,* No. 32 (May-June), pp. 50-53.

Groom, A. J. R. and Paul Taylor (1990). *Frameworks for International Co-operation.* London: Pinter Publishers.

Gwin, Catherine and Maurice Williams (1996). "The U.N. System and Sustainable Development," in Maynes, Charles W. and Williamson, Richard S. (Eds.) *U.S Foreign Policy and the United Nations System.* New York and London: W.W. Norton and Company, pp. 108-139.

"A Half-African Success Story," in *The Economist,* December 14, 1996, Vol. 341, No. 7996, p. 45.

Haq, Mahbub Ul et al. (Eds.) (1995). *The UN and the Bretton Woods Institutions: New Challenges for the Twenty-First Century.* New York: St. Martin's Press.

Harbeson, John W. and Rothchild, Donald (Eds.) (1995). *Africa in World Politics: Post-Cold War Challenges.* Boulder, San Francisco, Oxford: Westview Press.

Harrison, Paul (1993). *Inside the Third World: The Anatomy of Poverty.* 3rd edition. London: Penguin Books.

Hess, Peter and Ross, Clark. (1997). *Economic Development: Theories, Evidence and Policies.* Fort Worth, Philadelphia, San Diego, New York: The Dryden Press.

Himmelstrand, Ulf, Kabiru Kinyanjui and Edward Mburugu (Eds.) (1994). *African Perspectives on Development: Controversies, Dilemmas and Openings.* New York: St. Martin's Press; London: James Currey.

Hogwood, B. W. and Gunn, L. A. (1984). *Policy Analysis for the Real World.* Oxford, London and New York: Oxford University Press.

Holm, Hans-Henrick and Sorensen, Georg (1995). "Introduction: What Has Changed?" in Holm, Hans-Henrick and Sorensen, Georg (Eds). *Whose World Order? Uneven Globalization and the End of the Cold War.* Boulder, San Francisco and Oxford: Westview Press, pp. 1-18.

Holm, Hans-Henrick and Sorensen, Georg (Eds.) (1995). *Whose World Order? Uneven Globalization and the End of the Cold War.* Boulder, San Francisco and Oxford: Westview Press.

Houbert, Jean (1981). "Mauritius: Independence and Dependence," in *The Journal of Modern African Studies,* Vol. 19, No. 1, pp. 75- 105.

International Finance Corporation (IFC) (1997). *The Private Sector and*

Development: Five Case Studies. Washington, DC: The World Bank and International Finance Corporation.

International Monetaty Fund (IMF) (2002, April 15). "How Does the IMF Lend? A Factsheet." <http://www.imf.org/external/np/exr/facts/howlend.htm Washington, DC>.(Accessed on: December 29, 2002).

_____. (2001). *Madagascar: Selected Issues and Statistical Appendix. Country Report No. 01/219.* Washington, D.C.: International Monetary Fund.

_____. (1997a). *Madagascar -- Recent Economic Developments and Selected Issues.* Washington, D.C.: International Monetary Fund.

_____. (1997b). *Mauritius -- Recent Economic Developments and Selected Issues.* Washington, D.C.: International Monetary Fund.

_____. (1996). *Mauritius -- Background Papers and Statistical Annex.* Washington, D.C.: International Monetary Fund.

Jones, Charles (1977). *An Introduction to the Study of Public Policy.* North Scituate, Massachusetts: Duxbury Press.

Kearney, Richard C. (1990). "Mauritius and the NIC Model Redux: Or How Many Cases Make a Model?" in *The Journal of Developing Areas,* Vol. 24, No. 2, pp. 195- 216.

Kibazo, Joel (January, 1996). "The Mauritius Miracle," in *African Business,* No. 206, p. 12.

"Liberalism." (1994-1999). In *Britanica CD, Version 99.* Encyclopedia Britanica, Inc.

Lyons, Terrence (1995). *Somalia : State Collapse, Multilateral Intervention, and Strategies for Political Reconstruction.* Washington, D.C. : Brookings Institution.

"Madagascar: Country Report," in *The Courier* (March- April, 1996), No. 156, pp. 14- 32.

"Madagascar: Country Report, 2nd Quarter 1998," in *The Economic Intelligence Unit* (May 16, 1998).

"Mauritius: Physical and Social Geography," in *Africa South of the Sahara, 1997,* 36th Edition, London: Europa Publications Ltd., p. 639.

"Mauritius: Recent History," in *Africa South of the Sahara, 1997,* 36th Edition, London: Europa Publications Ltd., pp. 639- 641.

Maynes, Charles W. and Richard S. Williamson (Eds.) (1996). *U.S Foreign Policy and the United Nations System.* New York and London: W.W. Norton and Company.

Mazrui, Ali A. (1995). "The Blood of Experience: The Failed State and Political Collapse in Africa," in *World Policy Journal,* Vol. 12, No. 1, p. 28- 35.

Meisenhelder, Thomas (1997). "The Developmental State in Mauritius," in *The Journal of Modern African Studies,* Vol. 35, No. 2, pp. 279- 297.

"Miracle in Trouble: Mauritius," in *The Economist* (February 28, 1998), Vol. 346, No. 8057, p. 51.

Misser, F. (July 2001). Madagascar: Africa's Giant Island Awakens. *African Business,* p. 12.

_____. (March 1997). It's Now or Never. *African Business,* No. 219, pp. 25-27.

"Money Missing? Who Cares?" in *The Economist,* (October 14, 1995), Vol. 337, No. 7936, p. 50.

Mongula, Benedict S. (1994). "Development Theory and Changing Trends in Sub-Saharan African Economies 1960-89," in Himmelstrand, Ulf, Kabiru Kinyanjui and Edward Mburugu (Eds.) *African Perspectives on Development: Controversies, Dilemmas and Openings.* New York: St. Martin's Press; London: James Currey, pp. 84-95.

Mortimore, M. J. (1937). *Adapting to Drought: Farmers, Famines, and Desertification in West Africa,* Cambridge; New York: Cambridge University Press, 1989.

Morton, James (1994). *The Poverty of Nations the Aid Dilemma at the Heart of Africa.* London and New York: British Academic Press.

Mukonoweshuro, Eliphas G. (1994). "Madagascar: The Collapse of an Experiment," in *Journal of Third World Studies,* Vol. XI, No. 1, pp. 336-368.

_____. (1991). "Containing Political Instability in a Poly-Ethnic Society: The Case of Mauritius," in *Ethnic and Racial Sudies,* Vol. 14, No. 2, pp. 199-224.

_____. (1990). "State 'Resilience' and Chronic Political Instability," in *Canadian Journal of African Studies,* Vol. 24, No. 3, pp. 376-398.

Munasinghe, Mohan (1993). *Environmental Economics and Sustainable Development.* Washington, D.C.: The World Bank.

Murphy, Craig and Roger Tooze (Eds.) (1991). *The New International Political Economy.* Boulder, Colorado: Lynne Rienner Publishers.

Novicki, M. A. (1996a). "UN System Launches Special Initiative to Spur Africa's Development," *Africa Recovery,* Vol. 10, No. 1 (May), p. 1.

_____. (1996b). "Africa and Donors Agree to Intensify their Efforts for the Continent's Development," *Africa Recovery,* Vol. 10, No. 2 (October), p. 1, and pp. 4-7.

Nworah, Dike (1975). "The United Nations in Africa, 1963-1973: Comparative Roles in Education, Food, and Finance," *Geneve-Afrique,* Vol. 14, No. 2, pp. 83-94.

Nyangoni, Wellington W. (1985). *Africa in the United Nations System.* Rutherford, Madison, Teaneck: Fairleigh Dickinson University Press; London and Toronto: Associated University Press.

Organisation for Economic Co-operation and Development (OECD). (1998). *National Accounts, Main Aggregates, Volume I, 1960-1996.* Paris: OECD.

_____. (various years). *Geographical Distribution of Financial Flows to Aid Recipients,* Paris: OECD.

Polanyi, Karl (1944). *The Great Transformation: The Political and Economic Origins of our Time.* Boston: Beacon Press.

Prebish, Raul (1950). *The Economic Development of Latin America and Its Principal Problems.* New York: United Nations.

Pryor, Frederic L. (1990). *The Political Economy of Poverty, Equity, and Growth: Malawi and Madagascar.* Washington, D.C.: The World Bank.

Puchala, Donald (1996). "Reforming the United Nations or Going Beyond?" in Maynes, Charles W. and Richard S. Williamson (Eds.) (1996). *U.S Foreign Policy and the United Nations System.* New York and London: W.W. Norton and Company, pp. 229-248.

_____. (1995). "The Pragmatics of International History," *Mershon International Studies Review,* Vol. 39, pp. 1-18.

_____. (1994). "The History of the Future of International Relations," *Ethics & International Affairs,* Vol. 8, pp. 177-202.

_____. (1991). "Woe to the Orphans of the Scientific Revolution," in Rothstein, Robert L. (Ed.) *The Evolution of Theory in International Relations: Essay in Honor of William T. R. Fox.* Columbia, SC: University of South Carolina Press, pp. 39-60.

Ra, Jong Yil (Ed.) (1994). *The New World Order and the Role of the UN.* Korea: Ye-Jin Press.

Racine, Andrew (1978). "The Democratic Republic of Madagascar," in Peter Wiles (Ed.). *The New Communist Third World: An Essay in Political Economy.* New York: St. Matrin's Press, pp. 254-277.

Rajaonarivony, Narisoa (1996). *An Examination of the Impacts of IMF-Supported Programs on the Economic Performance of Low-Income Countries: The Case of Madagascar.* Doctoral dissertation, University of Auburn, Alabama.

Ramahatra, Olivier (1989). *Madagascar: Une Economie en Phase d' Ajustement.* Paris: Editions L' Harmattan.

Ranaivo, L. H. (May 18, 2002). "Avertissement des Bailleurs de Fonds: Le Prix de la Grève Sera Lourd pour l' Economie." *L' Express de Madagascar* [Online]. Available: http://www.lexpressmada.com (Accessed 19 May 2002).

Rapley, John (1996). *Understanding Development: Theory and Practice in the Third World.* Boulder and London: Lynne Rienner Publishers.

Ratsiraka, Didier (1975). *La Charte de la Revolution Socialiste Malgache.* Antananarivo: Impremerie Nationale.

Ravenhill, John (1986a). "Africa's Continuing Crisis: The Elusiveness of Development," in Ravenhill, John (Ed.) (1986). *Africa in Economic Crisis.* New York: Columbia University Press, pp. 1-43.

_____. (1986b). "Collective Self-Reliance or Collective Self-Delusion: Is the Lagos Plan of Action a Viable Alternative?" in Ravenhill, John (Ed.) (1986). *Africa in Economic Crisis.* New York: Columbia University Press, pp. 85-126.

Ravenhill, John (Ed.) (1986). *Africa in Economic Crisis.* New York: Columbia University Press.

Republique de Madagascar (1996). *Document Cadre de Politique Economique 1996- 1999.* Antananarivo: MYE.

Riggs, Robert E. and Jack C. Plano (1994). *The United Nations: International Organization and World Politics.* 2nd edition. Belmont, CA.: Wadswoth Publishing Company.

Sahn, David E. (1994a). "Economic Crisis and Policy Reform in Africa: An Introduction," in Sahn, David E. (Ed.) (1994). *Adjusting to Policy Failure in African Economies.* Ithaca and London: Cornell University Press, pp. 1-22.

_____. (1994b). "Economic Crisis and Policy Reform in Africa: Lessons Learned and Implications for Policy," in Sahn, David E. (Ed.) (1994). *Adjusting to Policy Failure in African Economies.* Ithaca and London: Cornell University Press, pp. 332-365.

Sahn, David E. (Ed.) (1994). *Adjusting to Policy Failure in African Economies.* Ithaca and London: Cornell University Press.

Sargent, Lyman T. (1993). *Contemporary Political Ideologies: A Comparative Analysis.* Belmont, California: Wadsworth Publishing Company.

Serpa, Eduardo (1991). "Madagascar: Change and Continuity," in *Africa Insight,* Vol. 21, No. 4, pp. 233- 245.

Shaw, Timothy M. (1986). "The African Crisis: Debates and Dialectics Over Alternative Development Strategies for the Continent," in Ravenhill, John (Ed.). *Africa in Economic Crisis.* New York: Columbia University Press, pp. 108-126.

Shepherd, Anne (1993). "Mauritius: Saving the 'Tiger'," in *Africa Report,* Vol. 38, No. 2, pp. 55- 58.

Simons, Geoff (1995). *UN Malaise: Power, Problems and Realpolitik.* St. Matins Press: New York.

Sparks, Donald L. (1997). "Mauritius: Economy," in *Africa South of the Sahara 1997,* 36th Edition, London: Europa Publications Ltd., pp. 642- 649.

Spero, Joan E. and Hart, Jeffrey A. (1997). *The Politics of International Economic Relations.* 5th Edition. New York: St. Martin's Press.

Stallings, Barbara (Ed.) (1995). *Global Change, Regional Response: The New International Context of Development.* New York: Cambridge University Press.

Stewart, Frances, Sanjaya Lall and Samuel Wangue (Eds.) (1992). *Alternative Development Strategies in Sub-Saharan Africa.* New York: St. Martin's Press.

Subramanian, Arvind and Devesh, Roy (2001). "Who Can Explain The Mauritian Miracle: Meade, Romer, Sachs, or Rodrick?" *International Monetary Fund Working Paper, WP/01/116.* Washington, DC: IMF.

Swatuck, Larry A. (1995). "Dead-end to Development? Post-Cold War Africa in the New International Division of Labour," *African Studies Review*, Vol. 38, No. 1 (April), pp. 104-117.

Thomas, Craig (June 1998). "Island Shakes Off 30-Year Dust," in *African Business*, No. 233, p. 38.

Thompson, Virginia (1997). "Madagascar: Physical and Social Geography," in *Africa South of the Sahara 1997*, 36th Edition, London: Europa Publications Ltd., p. 563.

Tudor, Gill (1997). "Madagascar: Economy," in *Africa South of the Sahara 1997*, 36th Edition, London: Europa Publications Ltd., pp. 569-73.

Umoren, Rose (1996). "New Debt Plan Sent Back to Drawing Board. Developing Countries Criticize World Bank / IMF Conditions; Creditors Refuse to Provide New Money," *Africa Recovery*, Vol. 10, No. 1 (May), pp. 6-7.

United Nations Development Programme (UNDP) (various years). *Human Development Report*. New York: Oxford University Press.

United Nations Economic Commission for Africa (UNECA). (1989). *African Alternative Framework to Structural Adjustment Programmes for Socio-Economic Recovery and Transformation (AAF-SAP)*. UN document No. A/44/315 of 21 June 1989, Annex, or UN document No. E/ECA/CM.15/6/Rev.3.

_____. (1983). *ECA and Africa's Development*, 1983-2008. Addis Ababa: ECA.

Urquhart, Brian and Childers, Erskine (1996). *A World in Need of Leadership: Tomorrow's United Nations: A Fresh Appraisal*. Uppsala, Sweden: Dag Hammarskjold Foundation.

Versi, A. (April, 2002). Madagascar's moment of truth. *African Business*. No. 1, p. 9.

Viotti, Paul R. and Mark V. Kauppi (1993). *International Relations Theory: Realism, Pluralism, Globalism*. 2nd edition. New York: Macmillan Publishing Company.

Waelde, Thomas W. (1995, June.). "A Requiem for the 'New International Economic Order' The Rise and Fall of Paradigms in International Economic Law," *The CEPMLP Internet Journal*, Volume 1-2 <http://www.dundee.ac.uk/ cepmlp/journal/html/ article1-2.html> (Accessed on: November 9, 2001)

Wallensteen, Peter and Axell, Karin (1994). "Conflit Resolution and the End of the Cold War, 1989-1993," in *Journal of Peace Research*, Vol. 31, No. 3, pp. 333-349.

Waltz, Kenneth N. 1999. "1999 JAMES MADISON LECTURE: Globalization and Governance," in *American Political Science Association Online* <http://www.apsanet.org/PS/dec99/waltz.cfm> (Accessed: November 09, 2001).

Weiss, Thomas, David P. Forsythe and Roger A. Coate. 1994. *The United Nations and Changing World Politics*. Boulder, Colorado: Westview

Press.

Wellisz, Stanislaw and Saw, Philippe L. M. (1993). "Mauritius," in Findlay, Ronald and Wellisz, Stanislaw (Eds.) (1993). *Five Small Open Economies*. New York, NY: Oxford University Press, pp. 219-292.

Welsh, Brian and Pavel Butorin (Eds.) (1990). *Dictionary of Development: Third World Economy, Environment, Society*. New York: Garland Publishing, Inc..

Wiles, Peter (Ed.) (1978). *The New Communist Third World: An Essay in Political Economy*. New York: St. Matrin's Press.

Wilkins, Gregory L. (1981). *African Influence in the United Nations, 1967-1975: The Politics and Techniques of Gaining Compliance to U.N. Principles and Resolutions*. Washington, D.C.: University Press of America.

Wood, Ellen M. 1999. *The Origin of Capitalism*. New York: Monthly Review Press.

World Bank. (2001). *African Development Indicators 2001*. Washington, D.C.: The World Bank.

_____. (1997a). *African Development Indicators 1997*. Washington, D.C.: The World Bank.

_____. (1997b). *World Development Report 1997*. New York: Oxford University Press, Inc.

_____. (1996a). *World Development Report 1996*. New York: Oxford University Press, Inc.

_____. (1996b). *Taking Action for Poverty Reduction in Sub-Saharan Africa: Report of an Africa Region Task Force*. Report No. 15575-AFR. Washington, D.C.: The World Bank.

_____. (1995). *African Development Indicators 1994-95*. Washington, D.C.: The World Bank.

_____. (1994a). *World Development Report 1994*. New York: Oxford University Press, Inc.

_____. (1994b). *Adjustment in Africa: Reforms, Results, and the Road Ahead*. New York: Oxford University Press.

_____. (1992). *Governance and Development*. Washington, D.C.: The World Bank.

_____. (1989a). *Sub-Saharan Africa: From Crisis to Sustainable Growth*. Washington, D.C.: The World Bank.

_____. (1989b). *Mauritius: Managing Success*. Washington, D.C.: The World Bank.

_____. (1984). *Toward Sustained Development in Sub-Saharan Africa: A Joint Program of Action*. Washington, D.C.: The World Bank.

_____. (1981). *Accelerated Development in Sub-Saharan Africa*. Washington, D.C.: The World Bank.

World Bank and UNDP (1989). *Africa's Adjustment and Growth in the 1980s*. Washington, D.C.: The World Bank.

Yansane, Aguibou (Ed.) (1996). *Prospects for Recovery and Sustainable*

Development in Africa.   Westport, Connecticut, and London: Greenwood Press.

Yunus, Mohammad (1994). "Redefining Development," in Danaher, Kevin (Ed.). *50 Years is Enough: The Case Against the World Bank and the International Monetary Fund.* Boston: South End Press, pp. ix-xiii.

Index

ABOUT THE BOOK AND THE AUTHOR

Adrien M. Ratsimbaharison attempts to explain in this book the failure the two major United Nations development programs for Africa in the 1980s and 1990s (UNPAAERD and UNNADAF). In doing so, he focuses on the processes of the formulation, adoption, implementation and evaluation of these two UN development programs within the UN General Assembly. He also analyzes the formulation and implementation of these two UN development programs within the context of the late 20th century world economic order. Furthermore, in order to concretize the previous analyses, he discusses the development experiences of two African countries (Madagascar and Mauritius) within the context of the formulation and implementation of these programs.

Adrien M. Ratsimbaharison received his Ph.D. from the Department of Government and International Studies, University of South Carolina, Columbia, SC. His is currently the Chair of the Social Science Department at Allen University, Columbia, SC, where he also teaches Political Science and History courses.